D1378690

MAN OF COURAGE

The Story of Dr. Edward L. Trudeau

Born: October 5, 1848

Died: November 15, 1915

MAN OF COURAGE

The Story of Dr. Edward L. Trudeau

By Kathryn E. Harrod

AUTHOR OF

MASTER BRIDGE BUILDERS:

The Story of the Roeblings

⬚⬚⬚⬚⬚⬚

JULIAN MESSNER, INC.

NEW YORK

Published by Julian Messner, Inc.
8 West 40 Street, New York 18

Published simultaneously in Canada
by The Copp Clark Publishing Co. Limited

Printed in the United States of America
Library of Congress Catalog Card No. 59-12762

To a
beloved physician and friend
HARRY A. ALEXANDER, M.D.,
Trudeau School of Tuberculosis, Class of 1929

ACKNOWLEDGMENTS

Of the many people who contributed time and knowledge to the preparation of the manuscript, I wish to make special mention of the following: Mrs. Francis B. Trudeau, Sr.; Dr. and Mrs. Francis B. Trudeau, Jr.; Mrs. Ruth Worthington, Librarian, Saranac Free Library; Mrs. Ruth West and Miss Marjorie G. Smith, Trudeau Laboratory and Library—all of Saranac Lake; Mr. Ernest Wood, former Superintendent of Trudeau Sanatorium, now of Pelham, New York; Mrs. Helen Wills Long, Executive Secretary of Zion Church, Douglaston, Long Island; Dr. J. Burns Amberson, Dr. Robert McCune and Mr. Hermann Huemphner of Cornell Medical Center; Miss Agnes Fay, Miss Mildred Nelson, Dr. Floyd M. Feldman and Dr. James E. Perkins, Managing Director and members of the staff of the National Tuberculosis Association; Mr. R. T. Townsend, Miss Vera Robson, Miss Eleanor Irwin and Mrs. James Alexander Miller—of New York City. The staffs of the Library of the Kings County Medical Association and of the Long Island Historical Society, Brooklyn; the New York Academy of Medicine and the New York Public Library were all most diligent in helping me search for material. Finally, I wish to mention with gratitude my editor, Miss Gertrude Blumenthal and her assistant, Miss Lee Hoffman, of Julian Messner, Inc.

KATHRYN E. HARROD

INTRODUCTION

The name of Edward Livingston Trudeau lives today because, learning by accident to live with tuberculosis, a disease which attacked him early in life, he devoted his efforts to helping other victims and directed his unusual talents to the conquest of a plague ranking first as a cause of death and suffering. There was no nationwide system of registering the cause of death in those days, as there is today, but we know that about 200 out of every 100,000 people in this country died annually of tuberculosis in the latter part of the nineteenth century.

Dr. Trudeau became the father of the sanatorium movement in this country. Today, the modern hospital has replaced the sanatorium as a place of treatment, but the "san," where rest was the keyword, was for many years the one hope of the tuberculosis patient.

Another of his great contributions was in medical research. Although not a trained scientific investigator, as we think of investigators today, he is credited with being the first man to grow the tubercle bacillus in an artificial medium in this country. This was the beginning of the Trudeau Laboratory, which is today an active center of research in tuberculosis.

In still another field Dr. Trudeau provided leadership in the fight against tuberculosis. This was the voluntary health movement, in which laymen and professionals joined hands in the early days of this century to bring their combined talents to bear against the greatest health menace of the day. Dr. Trudeau, together with Dr. Hermann Biggs, Dr. Lawrence F. Flick, Dr. William Osler, and others of like fame, was one of the founders of the National Tuberculosis Association (originally the National Association for the Study and Prevention of Tuberculosis) and was elected its first president in 1904. This was the first of the nationwide voluntary health associations which have played a notable role in promoting the health of the nation.

This period—from around 1880 to the early 1900's—might be called the beginning of the era of hope in the chronicle of tuberculosis. The tubercle bacillus had been discovered, the "rest" treatment of the disease started, a nationwide campaign inaugurated, and another scientific discovery of tremendous importance had been made. In 1895 William

Conrad Roentgen had discovered the X-ray, which has become indispensable in the detection and diagnosis of tuberculosis. It would have taken a vivid imagination to perceive where all these developments were leading at the time, but resignation was giving way to hope and action, and the road was being paved for the recent exciting developments in the field of treatment.

Today we have specific treatment for tuberculosis. Such drugs as isoniazid, streptomycin, and PAS (para-aminosalicylic acid) are extremely effective. Because of such drugs and new anesthesias and improved surgical techniques, it is now possible to remove badly diseased portions of the lung. Thus excisional surgery has largely replaced the collapse measures employed at the Trudeau Sanatorium and other sanatoriums a few years ago. The hospital in a medical center is now ideally the place of treatment, and this has led to the closing of many remote sanatoriums, even the Trudeau Sanatorium itself.

Since the day that Dr. Trudeau opened the "Little Red" in 1885, such progress has been made against tuberculosis that the death rate has been pushed down to less than 8 out of 100,000. Yet 2,000,000 persons today live under the shadow of tuberculosis in the United States. They are people who either have or had had the disease. Furthermore, almost 90,000 cases of tuberculosis are newly reported annually, and we conservatively estimate that about 40,000,000 Americans living today have been infected by the germ that causes tuberculosis. Of these, the chances are that more than 2,000,000 will suffer from active tuberculosis during their lifetime.

The job so well started by Dr. Trudeau and his contemporaries, and so well told by Miss Harrod in the pages that follow, has not been completed. Dr. Trudeau's life shows that the attack on tuberculosis must be many-pronged—that the resources and skills of the practicing doctor, the scientific investigator, the public health expert, and the educator are needed to bring it to a successful close.

And although we have not yet won our victory over tuberculosis, I am convinced that with the courage and vision of the Trudeaus of this world, we can do so. Furthermore, it seems to me that the progress thus far made against this particular infectious disease should make us realize that never should we view any disease as hopeless.

> James E. Perkins, M.D.
> Managing Director
> National Tuberculosis Association

April 16, 1959

CONTENTS

▢▢▢

I.

BOYHOOD

🔲🔲🔲

Thirteen-year-old Eddie Trudeau squatted at the edge of the Tuileries basin, tying a well sharpened long steel ink eraser to the prow of his small sailing boat. Behind him stood his brother Frank and Jim and Lou Livingston, friends newly arrived in Paris from America.

"There!" Eddie's black eyes flashed. "Just let those French boats ride into this. It will tear their old sails to ribbons."

Frank frowned. "How are you going to control it? You might rip the sail of an American boat."

Eddie was somewhat impatient with this practical observation. "Oh, I always hope for the best."

"Yes, I know you do." Frank laid his books on the basin ledge and examined the sharp steel point. "I think you should keep that in mind."

"Look!" Jim Livingston pulled on Eddie's sleeve. "Here come the French, ready for battle!"

"Step back everybody!" Eddie pulled his boat from Frank's grasp and prepared to launch it.

A shout arose from the French boys.

Lou called, "Hey! Come back here! Frank, one of them swiped your books. He is running, there . . ."

Eddie put his boat on the gravel beside the basin and whirled around. There was a splash. He looked up just in time to see Frank's strap-bound books sink into the center of the pool.

Lou and Jim raced ahead, and in an instant each was grappling with one of the French boys.

Eddie plunged into the middle of the scrap, collaring the one who had taken his brother's books. He pulled the husky boy's head back with the crook of his arm, kicked his legs and brought him to the ground with a heavy thud. Astride his victim, in an instant, he pummeled him with quick thrusts of his fists. The boy's nose was bleeding as Eddie heard his brother's protesting voice, but he continued to pound with all his might.

"Get up! What good will this do?" Frank said as he yanked Eddie's collar.

Choking, Eddie released his kneehold and got to his feet. He glared at his foe, "That ought to teach you. For two *sous*, I'd . . ."

At that instant two other French boys lunged forward, heads lowered. Eddie dodged, stepped back, caught the inside of one knee against the basin and lost his balance. He tumbled headlong into the water.

A roar of laughter came from the French attackers.

Eddie was furious as he climbed out, shaking the black forelock from his eyes and looking down at his pants which clung to his long, thin legs. "Let me get those fellows!"

Frank grabbed him around the waist. "Now, stop, Eddie! Come on, you're soaking wet. It's cold and windy. Let's forget about the books and go on home before Granny finds out."

"Oh, well, I guess you are right," Eddie said, still burning with indignation. "It's only that they are always picking on you."

Frank turned and walked toward the avenue. "Serves me right for laying my books down. I should have gone straight home from school. As soon as you get dried off, I will help you with your Latin. Exam's coming next week."

Eddie picked up his boat and books and followed his brother. Poor Frank had been born with a defective heart. Any kind of excitement was likely to cause his heart to beat irregularly and his nails and lips to turn blue. Granny would have a fit if she knew what had just happened.

The Trudeau boys were much closer than most brothers. Eddie, christened Edward Livingston Trudeau, was born in 1848 at his grandparents' home in New York—a fine red-brick colonnaded house on lower Broadway. Francis, or Frank, was four years older than he, and their sister Adelina was in between. Eddie could not remember her, for soon after his birth their parents had separated and their father, Dr. James de Berty Trudeau, had taken Adelina to Louisiana to stay with his relatives.

According to Granny, the Trudeaus were highly respected Huguenots, long resident in Louisiana. Eddie's father had graduated from the University of Pennsylvania Medical School and had studied in Paris before opening his practice in New York. Granny admitted that she had considered him a "fine catch" for her only daughter, Céphise, and was very happy when the couple moved into a house across the street from her own. All went well for several years, until Dr. Trudeau began to neglect his patients, going on long hunting and fishing trips in the Eastern mountains. In Granny's opinion, this was what caused a rift between James and Céphise, ending finally in their separation.

Grandfather Berger had a different explanation. He said that his son-in-law had injured his practice by making caricatures of prominent New York doctors—small, skillfully executed clay models which he displayed in his office, to the indignation of the influential medical men.

Soon after the separation the boys, their mother and grandparents, Dr. and Mrs. Francis Éloi Berger, went to Paris so that the boys could learn French and have the advantage of "good schooling" for a few years. Mrs. Trudeau obtained a divorce and several years later married a French army officer, Captain F. E. Chuffart. While the boys frequently visited her home at Fontainebleau, they continued to live in the Bergers' large apartment in rue Matignon, just off the Rond-Point and not far from the Champs Élysées. Dr. Berger was the third generation of physicians in his family, born and educated in Paris. Old and in poor health now, he practiced only as a consultant. It was Granny, Rebecca Aspinwall Berger, the daughter of a prominent New York merchant family, who was the real head of the household.

Although Eddie loved his grandmother, he was somewhat afraid of her. He was deeply devoted to his grandfather and was proud when people remarked that the boy looked like him—the same large-domed head, pointed jaw and low-set ears, the same brown eyes and olive skin.

Granny sputtered when she heard this, saying that it was what was inside his head that counted. She always finished this statement with a sigh, remarking that it was Francis who had the brains and desire to learn. "Eddie, I do wish you would study hard the way he does," she said.

Eddie never resented Granny's praise of Frank, who always came to his defense when she scolded. His older brother helped him with his lessons, taught him his Catechism and prayers and, when examination time rolled around each spring, crammed facts into his unwilling brain. Their best times together were in Grandfather's study on Sunday afternoons, when Frank would explain the wonderful pictures in the big medical books and make up games to play with the brightly colored anatomical chart on the wall.

It was necessary that they be together most of the time, for no one could predict when Frank would have one of his "blue spells." Then Eddie had to run for his grandfather or any other doctor who happened to be near. As he caught up with his brother now, he searched his pale, thin face for signs of strain. Even this little excitement at the basin might bring on an attack.

Frank smiled as they walked up the avenue. "I'll ask the concierge to let us in the back way. You stay in the hall while I find some dry clothes. Granny will never know the difference."

Good old Frank. He never complained about his weak heart, never seemed to envy those who could play ball, race or do any of the strenuous things that Eddie found so much fun. He seemed content to study or just sit and watch.

When the War Between the States began, many Americans, including the Livingstons, left Paris at once for New York. Eddie was sorry to see his friends go, for they, too, loved sports. Their parents were old friends of the family, and Eddie had been given his middle name in their honor. But Granny had no use for Lou and Jim. "I'm glad they have gone. They are a bad influence on you, Edward."

They were always getting into trouble at school and enticing her grandson away from his studies.

The Bergers remained in Paris, thinking that the war would end soon. However, it was 1867 before the family returned to New York, and Eddie felt like a foreigner in the strange, big city. Although he had studied English at the Lycée Napoleon, he still found the language very difficult. Frank spoke it with scarcely a trace of accent, and since he seemed much stronger now, took a job with Aspinwall and Howland, a mercantile and foreign-trade business owned and operated by members of Granny's family.

Eddie was too excited by the newness, the tall buildings and the gay crowd of young Americans to think about work. "After all, Granny, I am only nineteen. I will find something to do—give me time." He was sitting by the window, looking out of the four-story brick house the Bergers had rented on 20th Street.

Pulling her head from the depths of the trunk she was packing, Granny clucked impatiently, bobbing her lace cap as she spoke: "Honestly, I never saw the like. All you think about is a good time! I hope that during this long summer at Rockwood you'll settle down and put your mind on your future. I'll talk to you about this later. Right now I'm busy trying to get your sister Adelina up here. Those Southerners have had her long enough. When she gets used to our ways, I'll take your problem in hand, Edward."

Eddie sighed. "All right, all right! But if you ask me, I think Frank should have waited until fall to take this job. Are you sure he can manage with nobody but servants to watch out for him?"

Mrs. Berger looked thoughtful. "The doctor says Frank's heart is strong enough. He is so anxious to work. Yes, I suppose he will be all right. Of course, he will spend week ends up at Nyack with us."

At dinner that evening Eddie searched his brother's face, then asked, "How are things at Aspinwall and Howland?"

Frank's serious face lit up. "Fine, fine! But I'm glad when closing time rolls around each evening."

Eddie noticed a slight frown on Grandfather's worn face. Did he, too, wonder whether this job was a mistake?

After dinner, when the brothers sat together in the parlor, Frank said, "Guess who came into the office this morning? Lou and Jim Livingston."

"Wonderful! It will be grand to see them again. Where are they now?" Eddie asked.

"On their way to their summer place near Rhinebeck. You'll be seeing them soon. Poor Granny," Frank added with an amused sigh. "Want me to break the news for you?"

"No, say nothing about it. Once we are settled at Rockwood, she may feel more kindly toward the world. The prospect of seeing them would only get her excited now."

As it happened, the Livingston boys announced their own arrival at the palatial Aspinwall estate overlooking the Hudson River. The "family," including Uncle James and Aunt Maxwell Aspinwall, their children Minnie, Larry and Frank; the Bergers and Eddie—seated around the heavy carved table in the great oak-paneled dining room at Rockwood—were almost jolted out of their chairs by a loud banging of doors and several war whoops. In bounced Lou and Jim, their heads tied in handkerchiefs, their long legs covered with muddy, loose-fitting pants, their chests and feet bare.

Eddie observed the look of horror on his grandmother's round face as she shrieked, "Get your muddy feet off that Aubusson carpet!"

A ripple of laughter came from the young Aspinwalls, while their parents sat in shocked silence. Grandfather turned slowly in his chair and smiled.

Eddie jumped to his feet and threw his arms around his friends' shoulders. "Lou! Jim!"

"Shoo! All of you!" Grandmother went on, pushing the three boys out into the hall. "Now I suppose we're in for it!"

This was the beginning of happy, carefree days for Eddie, spent mostly on the river, away from Granny's critical and accusing eyes. He and the Livingstons rowed almost from one end of the Hudson to the other, sometimes stopping overnight at Grasmere, where Julia Livingston took things as they came, never complaining about muddy feet and soiled hand-woven carpets. The chief interruptions came on week ends when Frank arrived to spend his free day and a half.

Occasionally Eddie's fourteen-year-old cousin Minnie would insist that he escort her on a shopping trip in New York City. He rather enjoyed the novelty of wandering around large stores like Mc-Creery's and Lord and Taylor's, or going over to Brooks Brothers to select a cravat.

On one shopping trip, when he and Minnie met at Delmonico's for lunch, she announced that a friend would return to Rockwood with them. "I am sure you will love her. She's a wonderful young lady, just wonderful!"

Eddie was intrigued by the news. "And what is her name?" For the first time in his life he would talk to a strange girl without benefit of chaperone.

"Oh, didn't I tell you?" Minnie rattled on. "She is Miss Charlotte Beare, lives at Douglaston on Long Island."

All the way up the river, Eddie tried to talk to the tall, slender, serious young lady from Long Island, but the task was almost impossible. She replied, "Yes?" "Perhaps," and "You don't say!" to all his remarks, and he felt that there was disapproval in her large blue eyes. It was a relief to be nearing the end of the journey.

"It is such a beautiful day," Minnie said as they landed from the Tarrytown ferry at Nyack. "Do you think we should bother with a carriage? Let's walk up to the house. All right Lottie dear?"

"Quite."

Still eager to impress Minnie's friend, Eddie grasped her traveling bag and started up the steep, long hill to the house. He found it much steeper and longer than usual. The sun was hot, the air heavy, and he was out of breath by the time they entered the wide door. He set the bag down with a sigh of relief which he made no attempt to conceal.

Miss Lottie appeared to take no notice. She nodded briefly, then climbed the staircase, her wide black skirts a-swish, her handsome head high.

When she was out of sight, Minnie asked, "Well, what do you think of the wonderful Lottie Beare?"

Eddie rubbed his aching arm and shoulder. "I don't know what I think about her." He was feeling a bit grumpy. "I do know that she has an enormously heavy traveling bag!"

Minnie pouted for a second, then remarked, "You might as well get to like her. Everyone else loves her."

To Eddie's great surprise, he discovered that Lottie could swing an oar and manage a rifle with the best of them, and she was not afraid to ride the most spirited horse in the stable. She spoke admiringly of his skill at mark shooting and called him a "marvelous athletic young man." She even laughed at his clumsy jokes. She did not laugh, as did Minnie and the boys, when he remarked one day that the English language was a very hard language to pronounce. She nodded sympathetically and assured him that he would soon learn to speak without a French accent. How different she seemed, now that he knew her better. Still reserved, but reflecting an inner warmth and kindliness, she made Eddie feel that she enjoyed his company—which was flattering, for this girl was not the kind to make friends with just any man.

It was evident that Granny approved of Lottie Beare. When she saw Eddie trimming his sleek new black moustache, she remarked, "I think this young lady is a good influence. You look much neater these days." But he knew that she liked Miss Beare mostly because her visits kept him from spending so much time with the Livingstons. The first real inkling he had of her determination to discourage this friendship came from Grandfather Berger.

"I had better warn you, son," he remarked as he motioned Eddie to his cot in the corner of the wide veranda. "She has plans."

Eddie had a sense of foreboding. "What kind of plans?"

"For your future. She will tell you. It may not be so bad. My Rebecca is quite sensible—sometimes." The old gentleman chuckled and patted him on the knee.

Granny divulged her plans a few minutes later. Her first cousin, "Uncle" William Aspinwall—the owner of Rockwood—had connections in Washington and promised to secure him an appointment to the United States Naval Academy, at Newport, Rhode Island. It opened in late September, but meanwhile Eddie was to study at a nearby preparatory school so that he could keep up with the other midshipmen. A short month of work in mathematics, Uncle William's letter prophesied, and the rest would be easy.

Easy! Eddie thought of the gay parties he would miss next winter in New York, parties which Lottie Beare would attend, but he knew better than to complain to Granny. He told Frank about the plans when he arrived that afternoon to spend the week end, and was pleased to see the look of happiness on his brother's thin face.

"I envy you. But I am sure that I would never like the sea. Do you remember, Eddie, how sick I was even on our smooth crossing?"

If Eddie had wanted to protest against his grandmother's plan, he would not have done so now. He stood straight and tall, squaring his lean shoulders and trying to look pleased about the whole idea. He proceeded with the packing for his journey to Newport as if this were the fulfillment of his dearest wish. His amazingly expressive dark eyes revealed no trace of his sadness as he waved to the family from the train platform. There was nothing to do but make the best of it, he told himself.

He settled in his small room at the "prep" school, realizing that he must study hard—and by himself—for the first time in his life. There would be no Frank to help with examinations. The Naval Academy, he learned, was only temporarily at Newport; with the Civil War over now, it would return to its old quarters at Annapolis for the fall semester. So he made little attempt to feel "at home" in the town, since he would be leaving in a few short weeks.

Eddie had been at his studies barely a week when he returned to his room late one afternoon to find the door ajar. Puzzled, since he made a point of shutting it every morning, he glanced through the opening and to his astonishment saw a man lying on his cot by the window, his head turned toward the wall.

"Hello? What is this?" he asked, speaking French in a half-whisper.

The man stirred, coughed and turned over. It was Frank!

The next few days became a blurr in Eddie Trudeau's memory— the news that Frank believed he had "consumption," the train ride back to New York City, the arrival of his quiet, soft-spoken sister

Adelina from New Orleans, his grandfather's shocked grief, Granny's tear-filled eyes, Frank lying in the bedroom, coughing, tossing from one side to the other. None of it became real until the doctor arrived.

Seated on the stiff, horsehair-covered parlor chairs, the family listened to the quiet, matter-of-fact physician. Eddie buried his head in his hands.

"Yes, the boy has consumption—the galloping kind, I fear. His fever is a hundred and three degrees. He has night sweats, so you must keep all the windows closed, and avoid drafts above everything. He must stay flat on his back. I will leave medicine for that cough."

Dr. Berger glanced up, cleared his throat and said in his unsteady voice, "I cannot understand it. No one in our family ever had consumption. How could he have inherited this dreadful malady?"

The doctor shook his head. "Well, he inherited the taint from somewhere. It is not a disease you catch like measles. Maybe it comes from his father's family."

Grandmother grew tense. "That's it! Certainly. None of the Aspinwalls have died of it. I imagine that his Grandmother Trudeau . . ."

She looked so distressed that Eddie's heart went out to her in sympathy. What was the use in imagining? Consumption was incurable, the doctor said. Incurable? A feeling of fierce rebellion arose inside him as the word ran through his brain. "No, no!" he shouted and bounded up the stairs. It could not be! He himself would stay right here with Frank. He would nurse him, he would sleep with him, never leave him for an hour. Somehow, a miracle would happen. He was sure of it. His brother *must* get well! How could he write such hopeless news to his mother?

There were days during the next three months when Eddie thought that Frank was getting better, but always the bad days followed. His brother grew thinner. His fever was always high, even in the mornings. His cough was worse; he grew weaker and weaker. At night, when he could not sleep, Eddie read favorite Bible passages to him. They prayed together, they wrote long cheerful letters to their mother, they talked of their childhood in Paris.

Sometimes Granny insisted that Eddie leave the stuffy sickroom and take a walk up Fifth Avenue or down to Union Park while she and Adelina took over the sickroom. He walked and walked, hardly knowing where he was at times, eager to get back to his brother. "Surely something can be done!" he kept telling himself. But there was nothing, nothing. Even he finally had to face this fact.

Two days before Christmas, 1867, Eddie left his brother for the last time. His optimism, his strenuous efforts had been of no avail. His beloved Frank was dead.

II.

THE SEARCH

A few months later Grandfather Berger died, leaving Eddie with a double sorrow. He was now at loose ends. He had lost his appointment to Annapolis and could not decide what he should do next. To his great surprise, Granny's only suggestion was, "Get out of the house and enjoy yourself. You look thin, worn out. I will think of something later."

This was fine for him, since Jim and Lou Livingston were again in town, full of bright ideas, as usual. They belonged to a fun-loving crowd that centered around the Union Club on Fifth Avenue, and while they were not members as yet, their friend Billy Remsen was and gave them a standing invitation to join in club activities. Uncle William Aspinwall offered to add Eddie's bid for membership.

Eddie enjoyed the game room at the club where the young and gayer members gathered in the evening to play whist or billiards. Good at both games, he was by far the best in the crowd at billiards. Frequently the Livingstons invited pretty young girls to join the group for a new play or dancing at the Fifth Avenue Hotel, and it was usually well after midnight when Eddie returned home, exhausted but reasonably content.

That summer at Nyack was very dull; everything revolved around Adelina and plans for her marriage that fall to a physician, Dr. Charles Robert. The Livingstons were in Europe, and Lottie came up only once. When she invited him to visit her at Douglaston, he accepted eagerly.

Lottie and her father, the Reverend Charles Beare, lived in a middling-sized cottage on the edge of Douglas Manor and downhill from the small white Zion Episcopal Church where Beare was the Rector. Big, hearty Eliza greeted them at the door with a broad, toothy smile, and Lottie's father—a gentle, vague, round little man —trotted out of the study to add his welcome.

Eddie settled down in one of the soft, chintz-covered chairs in the parlor and drank tea, ate a dozen of Eliza's crunchy apple fritters and prepared to enjoy being the center of attention. Lottie was so unlike his cousin Minnie and the frivolous young ladies he had met through the Livingstons. She understood his confusion and grief at the loss of his brother and grandfather, for her own mother and sister had died of consumption. She was still in mourning for them. She treated Eddie like a good friend she had known for years. For the first time in many months he felt at peace with himself, but something she said one day toward the end of his two-week visit was most distressing.

"Have you thought of taking your brother's old job at Aspinwall's?"

"Heavens, no!" he replied, stalling. "That would be no challenge to me."

"What would challenge you?"

That did it. It was bad enough to have Granny looking at him with accusing eyes, but when Lottie began to prod him, well, that was different. In the following weeks at Rockwood he felt more and more guilty. He wished that he could take life casually, not care what Lottie Beare or anyone else thought of him. The truth was, he did care. More than anything in the world, he wanted Lottie's approval. What should he do? He felt numb and hopeless.

It was September when Granny finally came up with one of her ideas. "You like the out-of-doors, why not go to that new School of

Mines? A part of Columbia College, I believe."

Within a week Eddie was enrolled as a freshman at the makeshift old building between 49th and 50th streets at Fourth Avenue, but he saw immediately that he could never get interested in such impersonal subjects as minerology and geology, so he dropped out and started looking for a job in January, 1868.

In June, Uncle James Aspinwall came to the rescue with a position in a broker's office, but Eddie hated adding long columns of figures hour after hour, and frequently fell asleep at his desk. Finally he was fired. His next job was at Howland and Aspinwall, where he managed to hold on until late September. Again he was fired.

He came home to find that all the furniture, his toilet articles and clothes had been moved out of his room. "Where are my things?" he demanded when he found Granny in her room, calmly working on a piece of embroidery.

"*Your* things?" she asked, glaring at him over her spectacles.

"Yes, *my* things. You had no right to move them. Where is my property?"

"*Your* property?" the old lady snapped, dropping her handwork to the floor. "Whose money paid for those things? Do you think I will allow you to order me around in my own house? You and your paltry income of seven hundred dollars a year?"

Eddie had had many an argument with her over the years, but never had he seen her this angry. Well, he was angry too.

"You're nothing but a young sport. You couldn't get along without me or my money, and you know it. Your sister and her husband are coming for a visit. You will find *your* things on the fourth floor, next to the maid's room."

Eddie was now blind with rage. Why should he be moved to please a couple of honeymooners? Why didn't Adelina and Charles go on to their new home in Nyack? He raced from the room and up to the top floor. He dragged out his trunk, threw his clothes, brushes, writing set and framed pictures into it and slammed down the lid. Then he dashed out and started up the street, looking for *Room to Let* signs. Finally, on West 14th, he rented a fourth-floor bedroom for eight dollars a week, including two meals a day. He was not very happy with the place, but it was the best he could do. At Union Park he found a drayman who agreed to deliver his trunk for him.

It was all so sudden. His temper cooled while he was unpacking, and he began to collect his thoughts, wondering what he should do next. He was a failure at everything—in an office, at the School of Mines. He would probably have failed at the Naval Academy too.

When he finished unpacking, he sat on his trunk for a long time —thinking. His thoughts kept returning to Frank and the long months they had spent together in the sickroom. In spite of the hopelessness of his task during that sad time, nursing his brother was the most satisfying work he had undertaken. An old French quotation that Grandfather had often repeated to young physicians kept running through his mind: *To cure sometimes, to relieve often, to comfort always.*

It was a beautiful thought. Well, he was no doctor, but he had been able to do more than anyone else to help Frank over the rough spots. He had this much to his credit. The work seemed to come naturally to him. If Frank had been strong enough, Eddie thought sorrowfully, he would have made a good physician. Slowly the idea came to him. "Why not? Why shouldn't I try it? Yes, I will study to be a doctor!" He jumped up and grabbed his hat and jacket.

The only medical school he knew of was the College of Physicians and Surgeons. He had passed the old brick-and-stone building at the corner of 23rd Street and Fourth Avenue many times, with scarcely a glance. He looked at his watch: it was now three o'clock. If he hurried he would get there before the office closed.

He hailed a hansom cab and soon was climbing the winding stairs to the college entrance. The smell of creosote and ether greeted him at the door. As he stepped inside he saw that the floor and green-painted walls were sparkling clean, and he heard a chorus of voices around him. Something—certainly not the combination of smells— exhilarated him. It was the sight of young men in neat smocks with scissors, tape and pads of paper sticking out of their pockets. They looked so purposeful and contented as they strode from room to room and climbed the steep stairs. What a contrast to most of his friends at the Union Club!

He stood before the bulletin board near the office and read the notes that were pinned there. Under a printed heading, *Operations Today*, he saw a long list with Bellevue, Demilt Dispensary, New York Hospital and a number of others penciled in beside *Goitre*, *Ovarian Tumor*, and *Appendectomy*. He noticed that Dr. Henry Sands would operate at Bellevue; he had heard of him. Perhaps he, too, like his own father and grandfather, was one of the founders of the New York Academy of Medicine. Well, no matter. He must hurry to the office.

The College of Physicians and Surgeons was only nominally a part of Columbia in 1868, but it was a highly respected school with half a century behind it. Classes would begin the next day, Eddie learned. The matter-of-fact clerk at the desk told him that for graduation the school required three years of supervised study under a recognized physician and two full sessions of five months' intensive classwork. Most of the students also served in hospitals before taking their degrees. There was no entrance examination, he was relieved to hear; but the college expected the students to have wide knowledge of literature and some systematic study in science as preparation. Eddie had studied literature *ad nauseam*, but he knew that his course in science had been sketchy, at best.

"Bring in your credentials from the Lycée," the clerk said, "and if they are all right you can enroll. Meanwhile you might look at this list of faculty preceptors, men who will direct your clinical work and act as advisers."

Eddie scanned the list. The only familiar name was that of Dr. Sands. "I will take him."

The clerk smiled. "I am afraid that Dr. Sands has completed his list. He is an eminent surgeon, you know, much in demand. Besides, he takes only the best . . ."

Eddie winced. Did he look stupid? "It will do no harm to ask," he replied, trying to look self-confident but feeling that he was likely to be turned down. As he approached the doctor's office at the top of the first flight of stairs, his knees felt wobbly and he was tempted to turn around and run out of the building. But at that moment a handsome balding man with black eyes and a walrus mustache opened the door. He looked surprised, then his eyes twinkled as he said in a kindly voice, "I was just leaving. Want to speak to me?"

The prospective student lost his nervousness as Dr. Sands ushered him into the small room and motioned him to a chair near his desk. "My name is Edward Trudeau, and I expect to enroll here. I——"

Dr. Sands interrupted. "Is Dr. James Trudeau a relative?"

Eddie gulped. For one terrified moment he was afraid that perhaps this man was one of those whom his father had caricatured. But no, Dr. Sands was smiling. "Yes, sir; my father."

"Well, well. I knew him slightly. At the last medical meeting I heard that his health has been very poor since the war. Sorry about that. Sorry, too, about your grandfather's death. Only met him once —a great physician."

Eddie realized now that Dr. Sands was somewhat young to have been a founder of the Academy of Medicine. Where had he heard of him?

"You know the Livingstons, of course," the physician continued. "I mean the James Livingstons on Washington Place."

"Yes." Of course, he had heard Mrs. Livingston speak of Dr. Sands.

"Fine family. Now, what did you want to see me about, Trudeau?"

Eddie was glad to get to the purpose of his visit. "The clerk—that is—I thought perhaps, if you have not completed your list, you might allow me to choose you as my preceptor."

Dr. Sands nodded solemnly. "Oh yes, I see. My list is full, but I cannot very well send a member of such an illustrious medical family out into the cold. Suppose we explore the possibility." He rummaged around in back of a stack of papers on his rolltop desk. Out came two well-worn bones, yellowed and polished to a high sheen. Then he went to the bookcase, the bones clutched under his arm, and pulled out a heavy leather-bound book. "Now, identify these bones tonight. This book has all the answers. Learn the names of the parts. Come back tomorrow. If you pass the test, I will accept you as one of my students."

Eddie left the office feeling that he walked in sheer space. He hurried back to his boardinghouse, practically running all the way, then raced up the stairs to his room and plopped himself on his bed, laying the bones on the dark blue coverlet beside him. He took the book in both hands and glanced at the words printed in black on the yellow binding: *Gray's Anatomy—Descriptive and Surgical.* Inside, he saw that it was a new edition, printed only the year before, in Philadelphia by the Henry C. Lea Company, a name he recalled from books in his grandfather's library. Like many medical books, it was large, but this was larger than most. He leafed through it quickly. The book was set in small print with black-and-white illustrations—all clear and detailed. He consulted the table of contents. The first section dealt with Osteology, a word that he knew came from the Latin and must have something to do with bones.

"In the construction of the human body," the first sentence read, "it would appear essential, in the first place, to provide some dense and solid texture capable of forming a framework."

"Logical," he commented aloud. But what about these bones? "Take the easiest first, an arm bone, I will bet my bottom dollar."

On page 130, under the section entitled "Upper Extremities," he found what he was looking for—a drawing of "Left Humerus, Anterior View," and after comparing it with his specimen, he was sure that he had guessed correctly. But locating an illustration to compare with the paddle-shaped bone was more difficult, for he had no idea in which section of Osteology to search. At last he found it: "The coraco-acromial ligament is a broad, thin flat band, of triangular shape . . ." Part of the shoulder.

So far, so good. Now he must memorize the surprisingly long string of information about his new possessions. This proved more difficult. He had to look in his Latin-French dictionary dozens of times, then refer to his French-English dictionary before he could fix the names in his mind. When he was finally through he saw by his watch that it was very late—past midnight. He had skipped supper! He had missed his appointment at the club. Jim and Lou must be furious. They had promised to find him a date for the new play. Well, there was no help for it. He was too weary to think of going out, so he pulled off his trousers and shoes and rolled into bed, happy and hopeful. Tomorrow he would write to Lottie—if he passed the test.

III.

THE STUDENT

Eddie passed Dr. Sands' test easily, but the office clerk was dubious on the matter of his credentials. Eddie cooled his heels while he held a long consultation with someone in an inner room. Finally he was told that he would be allowed to begin studies at the college. He paid the entrance and first-year lecture fees and the charge for his work under Dr. Sands—amounting to nearly two hundred dollars. Also, he had to purchase several textbooks, including *Gray's Anatomy*, Loomis' *Lessons in Physical Diagnosis* and one by a professor at the college, Dr. John C. Dalton, *A Treatise on Human Physiology*. Although these last two were small books, they, like the one on anatomy, were frightfully expensive. He would have to count his pennies until he received his next payment from the Berger estate.

As he leafed through the new books, he grew more and more excited over the prospect. Was it because he really wanted to become a doctor? Was it merely the novelty of it all, something that would soon wear off? Or was it because this was likely to be his only chance to make something of himself? No, his desire to study medicine went far deeper than that. Strange that he had not thought of this before, while he was nursing Frank. . . . His mother would be pleased with the news. He must go home at once and write his weekly letter. This time he would have something important to say. Then a note to Lottie, matter-of-fact, of course. This would impress her.

When he finished, he went out to mail the letters, then walked up to the club to explain why he had broken his date and to share his good news with his friends in the game room.

"Where in blazes were you last night?" Lou demanded as soon as he stepped in the door.

"You got us in a terrible pickle with that girl," Jim added, pausing to chalk his billiard cue.

"Yes, I had to take the date for you," Ed Harriman said. "She was a humdinger. I thank you!" he added with a wink.

"Well, I got buried in a book," Eddie explained. He intended to break the news gradually, keep them guessing.

"A *book*?" The men at the billiard table jumped to attention as they chorused.

Eddie tried to look casual and spoke in an offhand manner. "Yes, *Gray's Anatomy.*"

A long silence followed.

"I have enrolled at the College of Physicians and Surgeons, and I'm afraid I will be pretty busy trying to make up for what I did not learn in school." Eddie began to feel uneasy. His friends all smiled and they looked him up and down as if he were an exhibit in a museum.

"Well, I never!" Jim exclaimed. "And you complain about being short of money. Whew, *that* will be expensive. Pure waste!"

Dan Moran began to laugh and, as he walked to the center of the room, said, "I'll bet five hundred dollars he doesn't graduate."

Ed Harriman held up a warning finger. "Not so fast, Moran. I'm not so sure about that. Eddie has a good brain in that large skull. Ever notice how he outwits us all at billiards? No, you'd have to give me big odds before I would take your bet."

There was another long silence, then Jim said, "Oh, well, you can borrow from us when you get stuck. A passing fancy, no doubt. Come on, Eddie, I will let you beat me. Get your cue."

He played one game and left. On the walk back to his boardinghouse he realized that he was now a part of an entirely new world, as different from the easy, lazy New York he knew as if it were on another planet. It irked him that, of all his friends at the club, only Ed Harriman took his plan seriously.

As he took a seat in the first row of benches in the fourth-floor dissecting room the next morning to listen to his first lecture in anatomy, he saw that the young men around him looked eager and happy. Several of them had Gray's text in their laps, while others held pencils and open notebooks. As Dr. Sands entered the room from a side door he motioned to a young man behind several rows of long tables.

The young man went out, then returned with a rolling metal table. He was a handsome, strong-jawed, red-faced fellow, all smiles and struts. To Eddie's amazement the students in the back of the room broke out into a chorus of catcalls and whistles. A shower of cigarette and cigar stubs followed. One of the audience called, "Bully for Bull!"

Far from taking offense at this silly pun, William Bull bowed deeply, smiled and, with the grand flourish of a magician, pulled off the table sheet, revealing a dissected human cadaver.

Eddie sickened at the sight and smell of it, but by swallowing hard and averting his eyes he was able to regain his composure.

Dr. Sands, dressed in a long black coat, his left hand in his pants pocket and two fingers of his right hand extended, called on one student after another to identify the organs of the body. It was evident that for many of them this was merely a review. Eddie was glad that the professor did not call on him. Some of the parts were so discolored that they did not look like the pictures on the chart.

At the end of an hour a bell rang and Dr. Sands left the room. A slightly built, mustached young man with wavy brown hair parted in the middle, seated next to Eddie, extended his hand and said in a pronounced British accent, "My name is Luis Walton. I see that you are new. So am I. Kind of nauseating, wasn't it?"

With considerable feeling Eddie admitted that it was. The two freshmen left together and walked down to the second floor, to a large lecture room at the back of the long building. Walton explained that this course on physiology was supposed to be one of the best in the college. Dr. John Dalton had advanced ideas and actually used live animals in the classroom. "Some of the medical men object, but he does not really hurt them—uses ether when he experiments, I understand."

The two students again took seats in the front row, and within a few minutes every place was taken. At least a dozen men leaned against the rear wall. Dr. Dalton was small and wiry, and wore thick-lensed spectacles. He bobbed along on thin legs, his coattails flying as he entered, raised his head high and looked out from under his glasses.

"Well, well, I see a number of familiar faces. Brushing up for the final-exam ordeal, no doubt."

"Hear, hear!" chorused the group of men at the rear.

"Very well," Dr. Dalton replied. "You are welcome, but I would like to see all the first-year members of this class in the front row."

As soon as the reshuffling was complete, Dalton began his lecture. "Now, as you must have learned during the first hour, anatomy makes us acquainted with all the component parts of the body, both solid and fluid. It teaches us the structure of the body in a state of rest. Physiology, with which we are concerned here, is a description of the body in a state of activity. It is the study of phenomena alone —not concerned with the *why*. Physiology can be studied only by observation. It is not like mathematics, where certain truths are taken for granted. I trust that all of you have had anatomy in your earlier schooling. If not, this course will be largely unintelligible."

Eddie groaned. Was Dr. Dalton speaking to him? His course in biological science at the Lycée had been poor. Worse still, he never looked at the book but managed to slide through because he was familiar with Grandfather's chart. From now on he must spend every spare hour reading Gray's book.

Many times during the next few weeks he felt completely lost. Dr. Dalton's pronunciation of the Latin words was far different from that of his grandfather and his Lycée teacher. Desperately he wrote them down, spelling according to sound, by ear only, then later consulting his dictionary to find the corresponding word. Frequently he sat up all night poring over the anatomy book, trying to keep ahead of the lectures in physiology. Fortunately Dr. Dalton was a brilliant lecturer, and he took nothing for granted, not even the preparation his students should have had in order to make his course meaning-ful. He used colored chalk to illustrate on the board every point he made. It astonished Eddie to see how much simpler these skillful chalk talks made even this complicated subject. The professor's ability to dramatize did not end here. As Luis Walton predicted, Dalton frequently brought live specimens to the classroom. This happened during the first week, when they were studying the nervous system—the second section of the text, which Dalton took up first, leaving nutrition and reproduction to follow.

"Open your books to page four-o-nine," the professor began, "to the section on the brain. From the chart you will see that here is the seat of memory, reason and judgment. I propose to illustrate to you that these faculties are not actually a part of the brain substance. The hemispheres are simply the instruments through which the intellectual powers, working through the nerve ganglia, manifest themselves." Here he stopped and signaled to a student in the rear.

The young man brought in a large wire cage containing two pigeons. Eddie noticed that one of them stood on its feet, calmly looking around at the audience soon after the cage was placed on the desk. The other pigeon wobbled uncertainly, fell against the side of the cage and flapped its wings, behaving for all the world as if it were drunk.

"Now, then," Dalton continued, "I have removed a portion of the cerebellum in one of these birds. The other I also operated on, removing its cerebrum." At this point a shot rang out in the hall. The professor pointed to the cage. The "drunk" pigeon appeared to be more uncertain, more agitated than before, while the second moved around sluggishly to the far corner. "Suppose you tell the class, Mr. Bull, which operation was performed on which pigeon."

Bull removed his cigar, uncrossed his legs and answered, "The one that acts like a drunken sailor is minus its cerebellum. The other is the one that had its cerebrum removed."

Dr. Dalton nodded. "They are permanently affected?"

"I do not know the answer to that question, positively, but from what you have said, I should judge not."

"That is correct, Bull. You judge right. In time the remaining parts of their brains are likely to take over the lost powers. We therefore see the result of sudden injury to the brain as a whole rather than to the removal of a portion. A clear demonstration that the faculties are not actually a part of the substance of the brain."

As the hour wore on, Dalton grew more and more animated, his voice rising to a high pitch of excitement, his frail body constantly moving, his eyes mirroring his enthusiasm. Eddie found this contagious. Could anything be more wonderful? When the hour ended he joined in the chorus of "Bravo!" that rang through the room. He left the class deeply affected, too moved to talk as he and Luis walked down the stairs and out of the building to the ground-floor drug and ice-cream shop where they ate lunch amid the confusion of smells—creosote, iodoform, ether, coffee and pork chops. The din of voices from the students crowding the small store made it impossible for him to hear what Luis was saying. He was glad of this, for he could now make notes on the lecture they had just heard —an hour so absorbing that he had completely forgotten to take out a pencil.

Not all of the lectures were as interesting as those of Sands and Dalton. Some of the men spoke in monotonous tones, as if teaching were an irksome sideline, but even then Eddie kept wide awake. Every sentence that was spoken, no matter how poorly phrased, contained real substance. He even enjoyed the chemistry course, although the professor did the experiments himself.

Lessons in the use of a simple two-lens microscope—the only kind then available—came early under Dr. Sands. In 1868 the college offered no course in bacteriology, a subject Eddie never heard of during his years there, although through the discoveries of Louis Pasteur and Jean A. Villemin his professors must have known that it was a growing and important field. Eddie was able to see more of the structure of various tissues, and the experience further stimulated his interest. One day, when he was examining a piece of lung tissue, he noticed a small nodule.

"That is a tubercle," Dr. Sands explained, "a manifestation of phthisis."

Eddie hated to show his ignorance in front of other members of the class, but there was no way out unless he waited to consult his medical dictionary. "I do not know what thy-sis is."

Dr. Sands spelled the word, then explained again, "The technical term for consumption—lung trouble."

Eddie stared at the tiny nodule. A tubercle. Phthisis! The disease he knew all too well. "Dr. Sands, does a patient have many of these tubercles before he dies of con . . . I mean phthisis?"

"Among other manifestations, yes. I don't want to go into this subject. You will learn about it in your course in pathology next year under Dr. Alonzo Clark. I only pointed it out as an abnormal condition." The professor moved on down the row of students.

After class Eddie cornered Dr. Sands, who listened patiently as the young student explained why he was so interested in what he had just seen under the microscope. "I think, now, that I would like to make the study of this disease my specialty."

The physician nodded, then in a kindly voice he said, "I'm glad to know that you have a genuine interest in medicine, and it will be of great help, a kind of spur in rough times. Do not expect to move too rapidly. This is only your first year and you must first learn all the basic facts before you even think of specialties."

Eddie was chagrined by this reproof, but he managed a smile.

"The first year is a real test for any student. Many lose interest; others lack the brains and stamina. Of course, some students run out of money before they complete their work. Well, I trust you can meet all the demands." Dr. Sands stood looking intently as he spoke.

Eddie thanked him and left.

On the way back to his boardinghouse, he took stock of his situation. He was grateful to his adviser for his frankness, but he was sure that, regardless of how monotonous any topic was, he would not lose sight of his goal. The announcement about wanting to study phthisis had come out spontaneously. Did he have the brains necessary to see him through the arduous three years? A good memory, the ability to see points quickly—yes, these he had. His weak preparation was going to be a handicap, and he must work harder than the average student because of it. He must learn to be patient, to be thorough. Stamina? Certainly he was strong, wiry, but as he compared himself to others—to the star student, Bull, for instance—he could see that he lacked somewhat in sheer physical endurance. As he climbed the steps to the door, he realized how very tired he was, and before he could sleep there were hours of study—*Gray's Anatomy* again.

Inside, he found two envelopes addressed to him. One was from Lottie, pleased at the news of his medical studies and inviting him to "come out when you find the time. You are always welcome." That was wonderful! He tore the flap on the other envelope. Out fell ten five-dollar bills. No message, nothing else. He looked again at the handwriting. It was Granny's!

With shaking fingers he replaced the money in the envelope and, clutching it firmly, he left the house. At the corner of Fifth Avenue he turned north and walked rapidly up to 20th Street. The light was on in Granny's room. He opened the door and tiptoed up the stairs.

She was sitting in her "lady's chair," embroidering as usual. She looked up, startled at seeing him. "Oh, it is you, dear. I thought you might need money. Medical school is frightfully expensive."

Eddie ran across the room and dropped on his knees beside her chair. "Oh Granny, you *are* good! You know about it? You understand?" he asked, choking back the tears and putting his arms around her plump waist.

She pulled him close. He felt her cheek resting on his head. "Never mind, boy. I miss you. The house has been so quiet since Adelina and Charles went back to Nyack. I fixed your old room, just as it used to be."

"Granny, Granny!" He could say no more.

"You will come back, won't you? That is a horrible place you have—so dingy," she said, blowing her nose on a small, lace-bordered kerchief.

Eddie moved back and seated himself on her footstool. "Granny, I know it is dingy, but it's the best I can afford. But let me explain: I am sorry I quarreled with you, but it did bring me to my senses. I cannot come back now. And please take your money." He placed the envelope in her lap. "You see, there's no turning back. I must go through with this. I can manage, if I am careful, without help until my next payment comes." He waited for her to reply, half fearing that she would scoff at his brave resolution.

A slow, pleasant smile spread over her wrinkled face. "It is just as well for you to try, I suppose. But if you really need help, well, I would hate to think that pride might cause you to change your plans. Julia Livingston told me what you are doing. Come, dinner is about ready. Let us sit down at the table like we used to, then I want you to explain everything you have learned at school. *Everything!*" She slipped her arm through his and they went down to dinner together.

Eddie poured out the story of the past three weeks. He told her about his professors, his textbooks, his new friend Luis Walton; he described what he had seen through the tiny glass in the school microscope; he talked about his hopes, his handicaps, the joy of finding a real purpose, of making a decision, his own. He was amazed to discover how much she knew about medicine, how frequently she interrupted, telling about his father's, his grandfather's early practice in New York.

"Eddie," she said as they left the table, "I gave you many personal things that belonged to your grandfather. I see you are wearing his silver pulse watch. His medical books are still in his room: you shall have these. But there was something he especially wanted you to have which I did not give you."

"There was? What could that be?"

She opened the hall cupboard and pointed to a tall mahogany box. "Just a week before he died, he told me that he wanted you to have his microscope. Naturally, I was puzzled."

Eddie lowered his eyes. "Yes, I know."

" 'I am sure that God will grant this last wish,' your grandfather said. 'I hope—no, I believe—that our boy will someday want to be a doctor.' "

Eddie was too overcome at this revelation to say anything.

"Do you know why he believed this? I thought he was out of his mind. But I know now that it must have been due to your care of dear Francis. You did more than all the doctors to ease him, Eddie. You have a knack for medicine."

It was almost midnight when Eddie returned to his room, exhausted yet happier than he had been since childhood. Lovingly he set the microscope on his study table and stroked its battered case. Then he opened his anatomy book. After a few minutes his thoughts returned to what his grandmother had told him. Dr. Sands had made many good points that afternoon, but he had omitted one important fact. A doctor must have brains, stamina, a deep interest in his field. Yes, and money to pay for his education. But he needed more—he must have a knack. It was a homely word; perhaps intuition, imagination was better. A man must have a knack to comfort the dying. "To cure sometimes, to help often, to comfort always."

IV.

THE GOAL IN SIGHT

Mrs. Berger continued to leave envelopes containing a few bills on the hall table at Eddie's rooming house. He always took these occasions to pay her a visit, eat a good meal and deposit the money on her desk. It became a kind of ritual that needed no comment from either of them. He spent less and less time at the club, since in order to make up for his deficiencies in general science and anatomy he had to study very hard, often to the point of exhaustion. Every other Sunday afternoon he spent at the Beare rectory, which he reached by rowing a small shell boat from its mooring on the bank of the Hudson down around the Battery, up the East River, through Hell Gate to Douglas' Landing near the manor, only a short walk from Lottie's home. These trips were like a tonic, and he realized that he had grown very fond of this girl. He was confident that she was fond of him too.

His chief weekday recreation was to join his fellow students in the stuffy ground-floor combination drug and ice-cream shop. The conversation always revolved around studies because all of these young men lived and breathed medicine. They talked about autopsies, lesions and various diseases as if they were the most interesting, even the only, subjects worth discussing.

The proprietor did not agree. One afternoon in the early weeks of Eddie's second year in school, he approached the corner table where Eddie sat with Luis Walton, William Bull and a few other members of Dr. Sands' group, holding a sign which he read aloud in an indignant voice: " 'No shop talk. Orders of the Proprietor!' "

Bull snatched the sign, held it at arm's length and said in a supercilious tone, "Very touching, very touching. Now, about that autopsy Sands did this morning. The upper left lobe looked like a piece of Swiss cheese."

The others paid no attention, but Eddie was amused to see the proprietor stalk away, muttering indignantly as he tore his sign to bits: "Decent people don't want to listen to this talk! Autopsies, Swiss cheese, ach!"

The young men gathered around the table that morning were about to hear their first lecture in pathology. Eddie was excited, for he knew that Dr. Alonzo Clark was the most famous professor at the college and was considered an authority on phthisis, or consumption, and he still wanted to make this disease his special interest.

Dr. Clark was sixty-two now, a tall, impressive figure as he stood before the class in the top-floor lecture room. He wore a curly, graying fringe beard, had deep nose-to-mouth lines and a thick neck which looked even thicker because of the standing collar that jutted against his ear lobes. Eddie thought there was an aura of cold authority about him, enhanced by his piercing black eyes now fixed on the students as he spoke in low tones, without notes, in carefully worded sentences.

"Our first topic for discussion in pathology, the study of disease and its effect on the human body, will be phthisis—a name given this greatest of all man-killers by Hippocrates. Phthisis, I need hardly explain, is a Greek word and means wasting of tissues. Hence, the popular term consumption. While we usually speak of it as a disease of the lungs, we often use the term 'phthisis' in reference to it in all forms, wherever it appears in the body. Phthisis is as old as civilization itself, perhaps dating from the time of the cave dwellers. About one in every five deaths in our New York hospitals is caused by this disease. The death rate in rural districts is lower, however. It is always greatest among the poorer economic classes."

After this brief introduction Dr. Clark directed his class to read several essays and books on the history of phthisis and trace for themselves the growth of knowledge and opinion on the subject.

Eddie took careful note of these references as Clark spoke.

"There are numerous theories as to the cause of phthisis, which you will find somewhat or outright contradictory. The best I can say to you is that we believe it is noncontagious, generally incurable and inherited, due to inherited peculiarities."

Eddie listened closely as the professor described the characteristics of the disease, how it develops from small nodules or tubercles which he had seen under his microscope. Then Clark spoke of the various types of phthisis, describing how it affects other organs of the body.

The young student was particularly interested as Clark described the symptoms of the disease. In the early stages, he said, the patient may suffer from one or all of a number of complaints: pallor, a dry cough, loss of weight, bleeding from the lungs, shortness of breath, tiredness, loss of appetite, sleeplessness and nervousness. Eddie thought back, trying to recall Frank's symptoms before his final illness. He had not had any bleeding as far as he knew. His brother had always been thin, but he did remember that during that summer at Rockwood Granny remarked that Frank must not be eating enough. He had been subject to chest colds which hung on, but so was Eddie. And Frank had always been a light sleeper. So was he. Grandfather had thought that in his brother's case nervousness came from his poor heart. Naturally he had been short of breath after exercise. It was most puzzling. Eddie wrote a question on a slip of paper and passed it to the front row, where Bull handed it to the professor: *How many of these symptoms must a person have to show that he really suffers from phthisis?*

Dr. Clark put on his spectacles, read the question aloud and replied, "All or none."

There was a low murmur of astonishment from the class. Eddie waited for further comment.

"At least in the early stages . . . Usually, the sufferer is not conscious of the disease until it is advanced. We do have certain aids in
diagnosis, however. Whenever I see a patient who is somewhat
underweight, pale or nervous, has a history of frequent colds, has
lost a parent from phthisis, I examine his chest." Dr. Clark pulled
from his pocket a jointed metal instrument. It had an open, flared
piece of metal at one end resembling a bell. "This invention, first
developed by the great French physician René Laënnec in 1819, is
called a stethoscope. In your clinic work you will have a chance to
use this instrument. The bell end is placed against the chest, between
the ribs; the jointed tubes fit into the ears. Through these tubes you
will, I hope, learn to recognize the sounds which are characteristic
of phthisis. They are called *râles*." Clark told how the symptoms of
diseased lungs become more evident as the disease progresses—the
cough grows persistent with increasing expectoration, afternoon
fever, night sweats, loss of appetite and weight, sleeplessness.

Eddie realized now that Frank's case must have been very far
advanced by the time he came to Newport. There was small comfort
in Clark's assertion that there was some hope of prolonging the
sufferer's life.

A few days later when the class went over to Bellevue, at that
time a great pauper hospital run by the city, Eddie saw a huge stone
building which housed twelve hundred patients. It was situated on
the east side of First Avenue, between 26th and 27th streets. As
they approached it, he noticed that it had one main range and two
end wings. A glass dome rose in the center; no doubt this was directly above the operating theater. The group entered through the
main center door, then walked down a long hall to the north wing
and into a large ward where men patients lay in long rows of metal
beds, coughing, tossing, with bright red spots on their cheekbones.
Eddie was nervous. The stuffiness of the room, the sound of the
hollow, moist coughing reminded him of the weeks he spent with
Frank. He felt impelled to go out in the hall again to compose himself, to get used to the idea; but he noticed that Clark was speaking
in low tones to a tall, dignified older physician whom he introduced

as Dr. Austin Flint, a name that appeared frequently in literature on phthisis.

Clark placed his stethoscope tubes in his ears, asked the patient in the first bed to bare his chest, exhale, cough then inhale slowly and speak the words, "One, two, three."

Eddie, Luis Walton, Al Little and several other students crowded around to watch as the bell-shaped end zigzagged its way across the shoulders and down the back. Clark repeated the process on the front of the chest, removed the stethoscope from his ears and, handing it to Eddie, said, "Well, Trudeau, what do you hear?"

It was embarrassing to be called on first and Eddie wondered what he was expected to hear on this attempt. After a few moments of repeating the professor's movements he removed the heavy earpieces. "I just hear a lot of noise—and a pumping sound like the heart pounding."

Clark handed the stethoscope to the others, one after another. Some of them reported hearing swishing, thumping, rustling and even whistles.

After that, Eddie and the other members of the group spent an hour each day with their stethoscopes, using one another as guinea pigs. They observed carefully when their preceptor pointed out signs of phthisis during operations or clinical examinations. Eddie was proud of himself, for it was evident that his hearing was unusually keen. After several months he could actually detect the peculiar sounds which meant phthisis—although only in very advanced cases as yet. This was encouraging.

He continued to search the latest medical books, and reread many of the books he had found during the first days of his course under Clark. One of them was by Benjamin Marten, *A New Theory of Consumption*, published in London in 1720 and considered a landmark in the field. It gave the long history of phthisis and all known theories as to its cause, beginning with the Greek theory that it was due to certain bodily fluids—perhaps phlegm—which descended into the lungs and caused trouble. It also listed a theory that it might be due to some peculiar atmospheric condition, such as swamp mist, an idea prevalent from earliest times. Richard Morton, an earlier writer than Marten, thought that the tubercles came from glandular swellings. Other writers attributed them to certain chemical or mechanical actions in the body.

Eddie read carefully through the long list of theories, and became more confused than ever. They were so contradictory. Medical men up to now simply did not agree on either the cause or the cure of phthisis. If only phthisis were more dramatic at its onset, if only someone could find its actual cause, then more scientists would study it. Regardless of what Clark said, he had doubts about its being hereditary, and in reading a new article by Flint, he discovered that this physician believed that it was caused by a germ! Flint offered no proof; no one had identified any bacteria which caused it. It was only a hunch; that was all.

Toward the end of his second year Eddie was talking with a fellow student one afternoon, commenting on the trouble the doctors at Bellevue were having in getting consumptives to take creosote and cod liver oil, the usual medications. Eddie became aware of the fact that his friend coughed frequently. "Do you have a cold?"

The young man nodded and went on coughing. When he stopped, he said, "Over six weeks now. The cough is worse in the mornings. I guess it's this damp New York air."

Alarmed now, Eddie placed his right palm on his friend's forehead. It was hot! "I believe you have a fever. Have you been losing weight?"

They were sitting in the ice-cream parlor, but Eddie immediately pulled out his stethoscope and began to examine his companion's back. He thought he heard moist crackling sounds at the apex of one lung. Or was he only imagining this? He could detect nothing unusual in other parts of the lungs. As he rechecked his findings, he decided those sounds at the apex were *râles*. It would be foolish to tell his friend about them immediately. First he would talk to Clark.

A few minutes later he stood in front of Dr. Clark's desk in his small office under the stairs at the college.

"Yes? What do you want?" the professor asked impatiently.

Hastily Eddie recounted his friend's symptoms and told what he had heard through the stethoscope.

Almost before he finished describing the sounds he had heard, Clark snapped, "Tell the boy to go to the mountains and become a stage driver for a few years. Good evening."

Eddie did not know whether to be pleased or shocked by this abrupt acceptance of his diagnosis. He recalled reading somewhere that physicians advocated a change of climate or work for people who had phthisis. Did Clark believe that this student really had the disease, or was he not interested? Out in the hall again, Eddie decided to ask Clark the next day to examine the student; but something happened that made him change his mind.

Dr. Clark was discussing dysentery and began by asking Alfred Little for a list of symptoms for this complaint. As frequently happened, he was not very kind to this student. "Now, man wants but Little here below nor wants that Little long, so make your answers as brief as possible, Mr. Little."

Alfred turned pale, stuttered, then replied, "I cannot answer."

Eddie was furious. A few minutes later the professor made what was an evident slip of the tongue: "In inflammation of this sort, ice injections into the bowels should be used."

No one dared to laugh. Eddie knew that Clark had meant to say ice-water injections, but still writhing under Little's mortification he slyly, under the cover of his notebook, wrote on a piece of paper: *What kind of syringe do you advise for injecting ice?*

When the question reached the professor, he glanced at it, tore it up and, after darting a sharp look in Eddie's direction, resumed his lecture.

After class Walton and Bull cornered Eddie in the hall. "It's all very well to resent his sarcasm and abruptness," Bull explained, "but you cannot afford to get on the wrong side of Clark. Better stay clear of him for a while."

"Just remember that he's the one who has the final say on who will practice medicine. You must get his recommendation to the board," Luis added.

Eddie tried to shrug off their fears. "Oh, by next year Clark will have forgotten all about it."

Bull and Walton looked doubtful.

"You have been kind of edgy yourself lately, Trudeau," Bull said as they left the building. "You need to have some fun."

Eddie decided that, on this score, the advice was good. Even with Sunday afternoons off he was not getting enough change of scene. He was not sleeping too well, and after observing Sands' operations he always had nightmares from which he awoke in a cold sweat. Sometimes he found himself reading the same page of a textbook several times without comprehending the meaning. So the next time Lottie announced that she was going to visit her mother's relatives on Bleecker Street, he hired a carriage and took her riding up through Central Park, along the Harlem Road and to High Bridge Park where they spent an afternoon hiking.

During the first of these excursions Eddie chattered about his studies, his experiences at Bellevue and his medical friends. Lottie listened very attentively, then said, "This is all most interesting, but don't you think you should get your mind off these subjects a little? You are somewhat tense, dear."

Eddie could scarcely believe his ears. She called him "dear"!

Nor was this the only time this happened. From that moment on they talked in more intimate terms, about themselves, their likes and dislikes, their hopes, their needs. She allowed him to take her arm and now when she smiled he saw a new tenderness in her eyes. He returned to his studies inspired and refreshed.

At Lottie's suggestion he dropped in at the club more frequently to play a game or two of billiards, although he seldom stayed long.

On one occasion in early spring he was too tired to think up an excuse for leaving the jolly gathering in the game room. The men were talking about a foot race they had seen that afternoon.

"Now take Eddie," Lou Livingston said. "Why, he could outwalk any of those guys. He is the fastest on his feet of anybody in town!"

"Last summer at Grasmere he outdistanced us all every time!" Jim added.

Ed Harriman, seated in a large leather chair with his feet slung over one arm, nodded. "I don't doubt it. He is quick as a cat."

Eddie sat there, leaning on one elbow which was propped on the edge of the billiard table, amused by this good-natured talk. It was fun not to have to think for a change.

Jim Livingston spoke again. "I will bet he could walk from Central Park to the Battery in less than an hour!"

Then Dan Moran hopped to the center of the low-ceilinged room and pointed his fingers to each member of the group. "I will take up that bet! A dinner free to all six of you if Eddie wins. An hour, I give him—one hour!"

Eddie was tempted to beg off, but something of his old pride arose in him now. It might be fun to take a brisk walk down Broadway. It would clear his aching brain. The walk would make him sleep better, then he could get up early and study with a fresh mind.

"Aw, come on, you old grind. Don't let your fellow club members down! You haven't joined in with us since you got your membership. Come on!" Jim said.

Eddie looked around at the expectant faces. Jim was right. He had been a member since Christmas, and about all he had done was pay his dues and eat meals here at the club. What was the harm in this walk? "Well, I am glad that only a dinner is at stake."

They left the club at once, piled into a hansom cab and drove up to 58th Street, then to Columbus Circle. Eddie got out and as his friends rode along, Moran with watch in hand, he started down Broadway, taking long strides, his elbows bent, chin up. It was a rainy, windy night, and the street was almost deserted. He noticed at first that a few people stopped to gape at him as he charged along in front of the carriage, but by the time he reached 42nd Street he saw only the long walk ahead.

"I am out of condition" he thought. His breath was shorter than in the old days at Nyack, shorter than it had been only last summer. These many months at a desk and in the library were beginning to tell on him.

Still he plunged on. He walked mechanically now, no longer conscious of his feet and legs. At 23rd Street he looked up at the sign. He wasn't even halfway! Or was he? The Battery could be ten miles down the island, for all he knew. No matter; he must keep going.

By the time he reached the Fifth Avenue Hotel in Madison Square, he was in great distress and gasping for breath. His face felt hot, his body dripped with sweat, his leg muscles ached.

"What's the matter with me?" he asked himself. He has been crazy to try this stunt. Would he always be a sucker for the Livingstons? And what would Lottie say? He was glad Granny could not see him now! She would take back all her kind words about him and his new-found ability to let nothing interfere with his studies. As for Dr. Clark's quiz session tomorrow night, he would be lucky to wake up in time to study for it. He winced as he thought how ill prepared he would be.

He walked on and on, in a daze now, aware of nothing but the wet stone pavement. The wide avenue stretched far ahead but it would be silly to stop now: surely he could not have much further to go.

At last he saw the Battery ahead. Just one more short block . . .

Suddenly his knees gave out; he dropped to the street, completely exhausted, not caring whether he had reached his destination. Nothing mattered. Then everything went black.

When he came to, he felt himself being lifted into the carriage. Jim Livingston was dancing in the street. "You made it! Forty-seven minutes flat!"

The announcement meant nothing to Eddie. He wanted to tell his friends to drop him off at his rooming house. Bother the victory dinner! But he was too weak even to protest as, with Lou on one side, Jim on the other, holding his trembling elbows, they triumphantly entered the Union Club dining room.

"All I want is a bowl of soup." Eddie dropped his weary, aching head and arms on the table.

V.

THE END OF THE ROAD

Granny, who had always seemed indestructible to Eddie, died suddenly soon after his "long walk." He felt very much alone after her death, especially since his mother was far away and he seldom heard from Adelina who had several children and was busy with her own affairs in Nyack.

Naturally, he went even more frequently to Douglaston, and Lottie now came into New York once a week, even when she had only an hour to spend with him. Without actually proposing, he managed to tell her of his love, of his great need, of his deep respect and admiration. And since Lottie was straightforward and sensible she asked no more. "I love you too, Eddie. But we must wait a while before we tell anyone."

Eddie understood why. His reception at the Grosvenors', her relatives on Bleecker Street, was always on the cool side, and he suspected that her aunt had higher aspirations for a niece with only a small yearly stipend of her own. They must consider him a poor prospect—no money, no assured future. "Yes, we will keep our engagement a secret for a while, but it's going to be difficult for me. I want to shout my love to the entire world!"

Lottie kissed him and then smiled. "You are so impulsive, Eddie. I love you for it though."

He recovered very slowly from the effects of his strenuous "walk," and in mid-April developed a swelling on his neck which Dr. Sands diagnosed as a cold abscess. After lancing it he said, "Nothing to worry about, Trudeau. I believe that it came from overwork and strain. You had better take things easy this summer."

Acting on this advice, Eddie accepted Mrs. Livingston's invitation to spend the summer at Grasmere. He enjoyed it there as usual, rowing, fishing, duck hunting and riding horseback; but when September arrived he was still tired and vaguely ill. Mrs. Livingston suggested that he go with her and Lou to the Adirondacks for a few weeks before school opened.

Lou was enthusiastic. "You'll like that wild, wonderful country, Eddie. Mother is one of the few women who has the nerve to go up there. It's a real he-man place, just what you need. And wait until you meet Uncle Paul Smith. All the big sportsmen in the East know him. Has the best hotel in the area. Quite a man."

Eddie had never seen the northern mountains, and the idea of going there intrigued him, although he wished Lottie could go along. He was amazed to discover that New York State was so large. The trip took two full days, going first by train—including a ride on an old branch iron-ore road into the foothills at Ausable Forks—then by rough stage to the Lower St. Regis Lake in the heart of the Adirondacks.

After arriving, Eddie wondered how any New York City dweller could have heard of this out-of-the way hotel and its proprietor, Uncle Paul Smith. This was indeed wild country. The air was crisp and cool, filled with the scent of pine and balsam. What a contrast to the heavy, smoke-filled air of New York! And the people looked different too.

The hotel stood at the edge of the large lake amid tall pines and was surrounded on three sides by forest, sandy slopes and rock outcroppings. One part of the large white frame building had four stories, but the second part only two. A long, friendly veranda faced the lake, and at the far end was a large boathouse jutting out on heavy stilts into the deep blue lake water. Men wearing leather boots, leggings, heavy turtle-neck sweaters and plaid shirts hustled around; some with canoes on their heads and shoulders, others leading handsome riding horses. Up on the slope behind the hotel Eddie saw two men working in an enormous vegetable garden. The lake was alive with sailboats and canoes riding gently in the soft breeze. He could see that some of them held fishermen.

"Welcome!" shouted a deep, jolly voice from the veranda.

Eddie turned to see a tall, spare man wearing a pointed beard, a broad-brimmed felt hat and heavy boots striding toward them.

"We have brought a friend with us this time, Uncle Paul," Mrs. Livingston explained as she introduced Eddie.

The proprietor's blue eyes were merry, and there was a pleasant twitching about his mouth as he greeted them, then led the way up the few steps, across the porch and into a large comfortably furnished sitting room. Eddie noticed that there were two billiard tables at one end. At the other, wide doors led into the dining room.

"Put another roast in the oven, Mama!" Paul Smith called out. "I can't let these city folks go hungry."

A small, chipper little woman emerged from behind a pair of swinging doors. "Well, I think there is plenty for everyone, Paul. Only thirty at supper." She dried her hands on her large blue apron and shook those of each arrival, smiling and saying "Welcome!"

A few minutes later, when Eddie looked out of the window of his fourth-floor room overlooking the lake, he felt supremely happy. He was glad that he had not brought any books along, although he had considered doing so. This would be his last year in training, and like other students he felt the need to "bone up" for the final examination next March. But here all thoughts of books, phthisis, doctors and exams vanished from his mind. It was like another world. Lou promised hunting, fishing and hiking, and "as good food as we have at the club, if not better." Even up on the top floor he could smell the roasting meat. He was starving!

What a sight it was a half-hour later to see Paul Smith at the head of the long table, sharpening his long, bone-handled carving knife with wide flourishes of his stout arms, smiling and joking as he sank the blade deep into the large deer quarter.

He filled a large plate with meat, potatoes and fresh vegetables and passed it down the table. "That one is for you, stranger. A doctor, they tell me. Horse doctor? We have use for horse doctors up here. Not the other kind though."

Eddie felt rather foolish. "I'm not a doctor yet, Uncle Paul. Just a medical student."

Smith passed the next plate. "You look smart enough. Still, I never can tell about a man until I get him out in the woods—take his measure, so to speak. There's no fool like an educated fool."

A few grunts of assent came from the guides seated at the foot of the table. Certain that he was blushing, Eddie began to eat at once, keeping his eyes on his plate.

After dinner another group of guests arrived, and while the Smith's three small sons were showing them to their rooms, Uncle Paul asked Eddie to go onto the porch with him. "If you like the outdoors, there's no place like these north woods. We catch the finest trout, shoot the largest deer and have the best fox runs in the world around this chain of lakes. Ever tried mark shooting?"

"Oh yes, at Grasmere." Eddie knew that the woodsman was already taking his measure. "The Livingstons and I went duck hunting a few times this summer. I like it." He resisted the temptation to tell how lucky he had been, fearing that this would bring a jinx on him now. He was eager to know more about this hotel. "Do many people come here?"

"More and more. I was brought up over near Lake Champlain, always been a sucker for the woods. About ten years ago Mama and I bought this house and began to take in hunters. Never have a vacant room during the season. We have about fifty out on camping trips now. Most of the folks are businessmen who can afford to come up for a month or two each year. My guides are all the best. They know where to find game."

The house door opened and one of the new arrivals rushed out. "Mr. Smith! There is no water in my room! Now, when I wrote for my reservation I told you that I desired only the very best accommodations. I demand . . ."

Paul Smith lifted a hand to interrupt, "See that spring house down there? Mama furnishes pitchers, no extra charge. Plenty of water for everybody. Help yourself!"

Eddie felt rather sorry for the stranger. "I guess that gentleman is not going to like these woods."

Paul Smith grunted. "See what I mean? He's a college president. Just like I said—no fool like an educated fool."

Eddie cringed. What did this famous sportsman-hotelkeeper think of him? There was no telling. In all his years of travel during his childhood in Europe, Eddie had never seen anyone like this man. He did not seem to have the least fear of offending his guests.

During the next week the guides took Eddie and Lou duck and fox hunting several times. The marvel to Eddie was the way the dogs knew their business. Those small black-and-tan hounds started baying at dawn, eager for the trail. Eddie resolved that someday he would own one or two hounds. Granny had never approved of animals in the house, so neither of the Trudeau boys had ever owned a pet. These dogs earned their keep; they were partners.

Each evening Eddie practiced mark shooting and surprised himself with his excellent aim—his eye was sure, his hand steady. The guides who had looked at him with apparent misgivings on his arrival now stood alongside, watching each time he lifted his rifle. Finally one of them set up a board with bottles attached and floated the target out onto the lake.

"Now, young feller, see what you can do with that," Fred Martin said, a hint of daring in his voice.

For a minute or so Eddie watched the board as it bounced on the wind-tide, then took aim. One by one he popped the bottles, never losing a shot. Paul Smith, who had come up quietly behind him, clapped Eddie on the shoulder. "I take it all back! You're only kidding when you say you want to be a doctor. A waste of perfectly good talent. You're a born woodsman!"

Eddie knew that, coming from Uncle Paul, those words were intended as a high compliment, and he could not help showing his delight. How beautiful, how restful it was here. He suddenly realized that all his weariness was gone!

The wonderful vacation came to an end all too soon. Eddie felt as if he were leaving old friends as he waved good-by to Uncle Paul, Flanders, Fred Martin and the other guides. He even blew a kiss to Mrs. Smith who stood in the kitchen doorway, waving her blue-and-white apron. He had never met such genuine people.

As the cutter drove out of sight Eddie turned to Mrs. Livingston. "I loved every minute of it. I'm most grateful Aunt Julia."

"Anyone can see that Regis agreed with you. Uncle Paul said this morning, 'I hope that young man comes back. I might even put inside plumbing into this old barn for him!' What did he mean by that, I wonder?"

Eddie plunged into his last year of training with renewed enthusiasm and a sense of well-being. With his class work completed, all his time was to be spent under Dr. Sands, his preceptor. It was fortunate that his income had increased since the death of his grandmother, for without that he would have been hard pressed for money. Now he could complete his year without having to borrow.

Better still, Lottie finally consented to announce their engagement in spite of objections from the Grosvenors. Several of Eddie's friends in medical school had married during the past year, but despite careful figuring he could not, so he was even more eager to complete his studies and open his practice.

It was customary for the students to plan for eighteen additional month's hospital service after graduation, but Eddie knew that one of these nonpaying jobs at Bellevue or the New York Hospital would only postpone his marriage. He talked the problem over with Lottie and later, at her suggestion, with Dr. Sands.

"I agree with your young lady. You need the added experience. Still, I understand your dilemma. Now, let me see . . . I just happen to know of another possibility. A Mr. Kaiser has announced the establishment of a small institution at the corner of Tenth Street and Avenue D in an old bank building. It will be known as the Strangers' Hospital and opens January first."

Eddie was about to interrupt, but Dr. Sands smiled and went on: "There are three positions up for competitive examination among last-year students. You will serve under me and several other doctors and gain valuable experience. The house-physician appointment will be for six months, the senior-assistant for one year. There is a junior's assistantship open too, but that's for eighteen months. Would you like to try?"

It would mean that he had to study for his final examination and work at the same time; still, the chance was too good to miss. "Yes,

I certainly will try, Dr. Sands!"

Naturally he wanted the job as house physician, but he would take what he could get. If he won second or third place, he would resign by autumn. He could not dream of postponing his marriage longer than that. Eighteen months was too long to wait.

His preceptor continued: "Now the oral examinations for these positions will be given by four physicians, myself included. I will give you the names of the others—all eminent men. Suppose you call first on Dr. William Draper. He's known for his work on diseases of the skin. Theodore Thomas specializes in obstetrics; Fessenden Otis in diseases of men. Consider yourself as having passed my test in general medicine and practice with flying colors."

Eddie left Dr. Sands' office in a glow of high spirits, but as he approached the office of Dr. Draper the next day, he was worried. So much depended on his passing with a high mark. The elderly physician put him at his ease at once, and after answering the first questions, Eddie was again self-confident.

He saw the other two doctors on succeeding days, after hastily preparing himself in each field as best he could. When the results were announced, Edward Livingston Trudeau placed first! He would be house physician, effective on New Year's Day, 1871.

His delight with this news was tempered by the fact that he did not know how much would be expected of him. He was to be in complete charge of all the wards! He confessed to Lottie that he was totally inexperienced in treating illness and injuries at the bed-side all by himself.

"Just do the best you can," she said. "None of the others has had experience either."

This consoling observation restored his confidence somewhat, but he was grateful that he would not have to take heavy responsibility in the surgical ward. The next two months were often more harrowing for Eddie than for the patients, or so he thought. When he arrived at Douglaston on his hours off, he was utterly exhausted from long hours of work and strain.

The Strangers' Hospital accommodated about 120 patients, with two surgical wards supervised by Dr. Sands and two for medical

cases under Dr. William Draper. In addition there was a genito-
urinary ward, a ward for diseases of women and an obstetrical ward
under Dr. Fessenden Otis and Dr. T. Gaillard Thomas. Eddie was
in charge of all the wards.

Not long after Lottie's remark about doing the best he could,
Eddie had a frightening experience. He had just gone to bed when
the night nurse from the women's ward rushed into his room.

"A patient has started to bleed—a hemorrhage. Come quickly!"

Eddie hopped out of bed, grabbed his dressing gown and ran
downstairs and into the ward. As he entered he saw a stream of
blood running across the floor from under one bed. He managed to
cry out, "Get a pan of cold water, some ice, cloths, hurry!"

All of the patients were awake now, some of them out of their
beds, some weeping, others rushing around trying to mop up the
blood. As soon as the nurse returned with the water and ice, he
dipped the cloths in the pan, placed them on the patient's chest
and said in as soothing a tone as he could muster, "You'll be all
right. Lie as still as you can."

After a few minutes the flow of blood became a trickle and finally
stopped. Eddie sighed with relief as he nodded to the nurse. "You
can clean her up now, but keep the poultices on until morning.
Change them every time they get warm. Call if you need me."

As he left the ward he was pleased that things were under control,
and the next day Dr. Draper congratulated him on his presence of
mind.

Examination time arrived all too soon, since he had no time to
study for the ordeal. Like the examinations he had taken a few
months earlier, this was oral and given by Dr. Alonzo Clark under
the auspices of the County Medical Society, which would award the
diplomas. Eddie was trembling with fear when his turn arrived. He
found the old professor sitting in his dusty office, a fur-lined coat
on his knees. He showed no signs of recognition but looked down
his list of students' names.

Eddie was anxious to get on pleasant terms immediately, so he
said, in the cheeriest tone he could manage, "My name is Trudeau,

sir." After all, Clark *could* have forgotten—or could he?

"I know it."

A long, long pause.

"Mr. Trudeau, what is pain a symptom of?" The question came out like a gunshot as the physician glared from under bushy brows.

Eddie swallowed hard, hesitating an instant in order to gain control of his voice.

"Mr. Trudeau, have you forgotten? Or did you ever learn?"

Eddie gulped again. He had not expected such a sweeping question, and it took another moment for him to start down the long list of inflammations, neuralgias and injuries which cause pain. Finally, when he had named all he could think of, there was a long silence.

"Mr. Trudeau, you have omitted one long pain."

Frantically the student pulled from the back of his brain—he never knew how—the word "sciatica."

The questions came faster. "Mr. Trudeau, what is a lung hemorrhage a symptom of?"

"Phthisis!" Eddie was quite sure of himself this time.

"What is fever a symptom of, Mr. Trudeau?"

It seemed to Eddie that there was unusually strong emphasis on the word "Mister." There could be no doubt that Clark was trying to put him in a corner, make him lose his presence of mind. Eddie was determined that this would not happen.

If there was any disease of the human body, any malfunction, any subject in the field of medical practice that Dr. Clark failed to cover during this, the longest two hours of Eddie's life, the student was not aware of it. As he left the office, weak and dazed, he met Luis Walton, waiting his turn in the hall.

"How was it?" his friend asked, looking rather fearful.

"Well"—Eddie was a bit amused now—"the only question he did not ask was what kind of syringe I would use for injecting ice!"

"Whew! The old boy never forgets, does he?"

"Apparently not."

"Do you think you passed?"

Eddie shrugged. "I—I think so, still . . ."

Eddie waited in the office next door for Luis. He came out after just forty-five minutes, looking tired but happy. "He was not very hard on me. Must have shot his bolt with you, Trudeau."

Strangely, after the ordeal of the examination and the week of waiting for the results to be posted on the bulletin board, the actual awarding of diplomas was an anticlimax to Eddie. Until he saw Lottie's beaming face outside the lecture hall he did not realize what it all meant.

"Congratulations, Dr. Edward Livingston Trudeau!" she called as she hurried toward him.

He grasped both her hands and looked into her eyes. "It sounds wonderful, doesn't it? Just think what it means, Lottie, to hear you call me Doctor."

All the pent-up emotion, all memories of the long waiting and uncertainty came over him now. He had come to the end of the long road! At last he had that sheepskin, lettered in Latin, the first concrete evidence that he was a physician, entitled to practice on his own. All the joy, the relief, the pride and realization that this was true welled up in his heart. "God has been good to me!" he whispered.

"He has been good to both of us," Lottie said as they walked, arm in arm, out of the building.

VI.

A STRANGE TURNING

Dr. Edward Livingston Trudeau and Miss Charlotte Grosvenor Beare were married on June 29, 1871, by the young lady's father, in Zion Episcopal Church. "Everyone" was there, including the rich and poor of Douglaston, the Livingstons, the Aspinwall relatives, the Union Club crowd, and sister Adelina with her husband, Dr. Charles

Robert. Willie Douglas, who owned the manor and was unofficial mayor of the village, took charge of the reception at his beautiful white house on a wooded slope above the bay at Little Neck.

Young Dr. and Mrs. Trudeau spent a few happy weeks in the White Mountains, then sailed for Europe on the Cunard liner *Russia*. It was Lottie's first trip abroad, and she expressed her eagerness to see all of Eddie's old haunts.

After short stays in Switzerland and Germany they went to France. Eddie grew more and more excited as the train pulled into the Paris station. The city was just as he remembered it, the crowds on the platform, the blue-smocked porters in their black-visored caps juggling huge bags and trunks. Eagerly he searched faces as he and Lottie descended from their compartment. Far in the rear he spotted a small, slender woman wearing a tiny hat covered with blue flowers. "Mama!" He dropped Lottie's hand and pushed his way through the crowd. "Oh, it is good to see you again!"

"My boy! My darling boy!" She kissed him several times on each cheek, then held him at arm's length. "Why, you are a man!"

Eddie laughed his delight. Tears of joy came to his eyes. "Yes, little Mama, I am a man and a *doctor!*"

Madame Chuffart had a ringing laugh that rose to a high soprano. "But yes, of course! Dr. Trudeau!"

Lottie stood by, silently waiting to be introduced. She smiled graciously and shook hands with Eddie's mother, then bent her head for a kiss.

Lottie said little during the long ride to Fontainebleau, although she smiled and answered her mother-in-law's questions which were sandwiched into Eddie's excited chatter.

When they reached the house, Madame Chuffart and her son regained some of their composure. It was a nice, cozy place, with a flower garden in front, surrounded by a high wall—a typical French villa, shuttered, of gray cement with dark green trim. As they entered, Eddie's mother explained that her husband was in England at the moment. "So you see, we shall have plenty of time for getting acquainted. Oh Eddie, your girl is perfect! I can see that. You were always the lucky one!" And she reached up to put her arms around Lottie's neck. "Everything works out well for Eddie. It is always so!"

"Naturally, I expect it to!" Eddie retorted, laughing.

This was a happy week for him. It was truly remarkable to see how well these two women got on together, although they were not at all alike—Lottie so tall, dignified and quiet, his mother small, quick in movement like himself, bubbling with talk. She seemed more French than he remembered her.

One day she spoke of his father. "I had a letter from James' sister a month ago. She said that he was still in miserable health. He was seriously injured in the war, you know. But he's trying to practice. Poor man, I'm glad that Adelina writes to him. Do you suppose he knows about your being a physician?"

The thought had not occurred to Eddie. He could not remember his father. If he were curious, certainly he would write to his own son. Eddie could see no reason why he should begin a correspondence with a perfect stranger, even though he was his father. "I am sure that Adelina will tell him," he said, shrugging his shoulders.

His mother looked at him sharply for a second, then smiled and said brightly, "Oh, it was grand to see that girl. And I liked her solemn husband too! They stayed a whole month with me on *their* honeymoon."

Eddie felt uneasy when he heard this. This week had gone too fast for all of them. If he were not so eager to get back to work, he would suggest to Lottie that they prolong their visit.

They spent their last day in Paris where Lottie had her first glimpse of rue Matignon. The fine apartment house looked just as it had during Eddie's boyhood. The concierge, now a feeble old man, did not recognize his former tenant, but when he heard the name he clapped his knees and shook his head in bewilderment. "It is impossible, *mais oui!* Ah, and to think you were the naughtiest, the worst of them all!"

They had a good laugh at this remark; it was all great fun. However, Eddie was conscious of not feeling well; perhaps it was due to excitement. But his neck glands were swollen again, and he pointed this out to Lottie. She was alarmed and insisted that he see a physician as soon as they reached London. He thought this was silly but followed her urging merely to please her.

The diagnosis was the same as Dr. Sands' earlier one—Eddie was only tired. "Eat plenty of bacon to put on weight. Paint your neck with iodine and take a tonic with iron in it. You will be all right soon. By the way, you may be smoking too much."

Eddie ignored this remark. "You see, Lottie? It is nothing, just the same trouble I had in New York."

The return boat trip did not help, for the sea was stormy and so rough that the crossing took two weeks. Eddie noticed that Lottie stood the bad weather much better than he did. Nothing fazed her until the vessel started to ship water and their stateroom floor became so flooded that they had to stand on the couch to keep their feet dry. Thoroughly frightened, he looked at Lottie. Although her eyes showed real concern, her only indication of it came when he lifted their steamer trunk into the upper berth:

"What did you do that for? We'll never need it again."

More worried than ever, Eddie ran out into the flooded passageway to find the steward. "Is the ship going to the bottom?" he called.

The steward looked surprised, then a broad grin spread across his jovial face. "Why, don't you know you can't sink a Cunarder?"

Eddie, feeling rather foolish, hurried back to the cabin to reassure Lottie who was sitting on the couch, her feet tucked under her.

He learned one important fact from this harrowing experience on the *China*: his Lottie had what it took to live through anything. And when the sea calmed she appeared to forget the danger they had faced. She never spoke of it again.

Until now Eddie had had no definite plans for his practice, except for his determination to specialize in the treatment of phthisis— eventually. He could not expect to do this at once, for professional as well as financial reasons. Physicians and even the public frowned on narrow specialization in one so new in the profession. A few years of general practice were essential. So when Willie Douglas offered the young couple a small gate cottage at the manor, promising to use his influence in the community to get the new doctor started, the Trudeaus gladly accepted. They both loved the country, and of course the Reverend Beare was delighted to have them nearby, for the old parsonage was a lonely place, even with the faithful Eliza to look after him.

At first Eddie believed that the decision to stay at Little Neck was the best he could have made. The slow pace, the restful drives through the wooded lanes to call on his patients soon restored him. Lottie again played the melodeon at the church, and he received an appointment as vestryman. It was like the old days in Paris, when he and Frank went to the American chapel for Sunday services.

Zion's rectangular room, with light streaming through the trees into the tall windows, was restful and beautiful and the services always well attended. Willie Douglas came, and James Gordon Bennett, the publisher of the New York *Herald*. Poet William Cullen Bryant came over from Roslyn. It was a simple service, yet in High Church tradition.

Eddie told himself that no young physician could ask for a better place to start on a career—yet he was vaguely dissatisfied. He said nothing for a time to Lottie since her hands were full trying to help her father and still manage her own household. But after their first baby, named Charlotte for her mother but called Chatte, instead of Lottie, was born April 23, 1872, Eddie resolved to make a change. Most of his practice was humdrum—nearly everyone along the marshy coast had malaria, for which he could only prescribe quinine. No one knew what caused it. There were only a few cases of phthisis. Since he was the only doctor in the area, he had frequent night calls, leaving little time to study the medical periodicals and none at all to go into New York for consultation with other physicians. He would go to seed at this rate.

An incident occurred that summer which brought his decision into the open. There never was a better man, a more trusting soul, a more impractical mind than Reverend Beare. For two years the community had been aroused because someone was stealing valuable possessions. Local families lost silver, jewelry and carpets. Even the church floor coverings and altar linen disappeared.

"Why don't you call the police?" Eddie asked one day when his father-in-law was complaining about a new outbreak of theft.

"The police? Oh dear no, that would make a scandal! No one here in Douglaston would *steal*," the Reverend Beare protested.

Weary of the long discussion, Eddie snapped, "Well, *somebody* is stealing and right under your nose!"

Late that evening when he was returning from a call at Great Neck, he happened to notice a light in the belfry tower. A minute later out came the sexton, Jefferson Knight. Eddie waited. This was a queer time for the sexton to be coming out of the church. After Knight was gone, Eddie drove up the hill, tied his horse to the hitching post and climbed the steep stairs to the belfry. He found cooking utensils, a pair of bellows from an old organ, iron pots and a small furnace. So that was where the silver went—it was melted in this furnace!

He drove at once to the police station and reported his discovery. A few days later the story came out: the sexton was a member of a gang who had burglarized the neighbors while they were at church. Several of the men had actually slept in the belfry, taking the results of their plunder by boat into New York by night.

Eddie was called to testify in court about all this and spent many hours repeating his story to parishioners—all time wasted as far as his practice was concerned.

"I can see that you are unhappy," Lottie said when the excitement died down. "Father has come to lean on you. We made a mistake in settling here."

Grateful to her for this understanding observation, Eddie confessed that for some time he had been dissatisfied.

When Reverend Beare heard of their decision to leave, he accepted it with good grace. "I was afraid this would happen. Well, it has been a good year."

Now that they were all agreed, Eddie faced his problem squarely. The fact that he had little money should not stop him from moving to New York. He returned from a hasty inspection trip bubbling over with enthusiasm. Everything was settled: "We will live on our capital while I get started. Luis found a nice house on West Forty-sixth Street, just off Fifth Avenue. The rent will be low because there is a livery stable next door. The owner offered me a three-year lease. I could not get a better location for my practice."

The Trudeaus moved into the city a month later. Lottie had a flair for making any place homelike and soon they were cozy and happy in the small, sixteen-foot-wide house. Eddie joined Dr. Luis Walton at the Demilt Dispensary where they shared a class for medical students in diseases of the chest.

Demilt Dispensary was one of a group of out-patient clinics located in the more populous sections of the city. It was a three-story brick building, of neo-Gothic design, at the corner of Second Avenue and 23rd Street. Consumptives who were considered well enough to live at home came to Demilt for periodic examinations; and since this was the most prevalent of all diseases, Eddie and Luis had to have a number of student assistants. It was to this group that the two doctors lectured, frequently demonstrating techniques of auscultation by ear, also using the stethoscope and a small rubber hammer to tap the patient's chest. Since there were as many as ten thousand visitors a year to the clinic at this time, over half of them consumptive, it was excellent experience for the doctors as well as their students.

Trudeau saw cases of chest tumor, asthma, pneumonia and malformation, and soon became skilled at detecting them. Tumors had to be referred to surgery, but they were rare. As the weeks passed he worried because there was so little he could do for these sufferers. Creosote, cod liver oil and cough medicine were still the usual prescriptions. They had not changed since the days of Frank's illness. And as Eddie talked with the patients, taking down their life histories, he learned that they all lived in crowded tenements, frequently with little to eat, and every single one of them had financial or other family worries. It was very depressing. He spent two days a week at the Bellevue clinic, learning all he could from the noted chest specialist, Dr. Austin Flint. Even though he could offer little hope to the sick, he felt that he was at least gaining valuable experience and skill. Dr. Flint and the diagnostician Dr. Edward Janeway complimented him on his ability to detect phthisis in its early stages.

Then another stroke of good fortune came along. Dr. Fessenden Otis, under whom he had worked at the Strangers' Hospital, asked him to take a few of his calls and share the fees. Otis was a specialist in diseases of men, but there was no reason why a young doctor could not make good use of this added experience. It would mean more money too.

Eddie now looked on himself as the luckiest and happiest man in the world. He had every reason to look forward to a fine practice, a good reputation among his peers and a perfect family life. His daughter Chatte was strong and handsome, calm and good-natured like her mother, and another baby was on the way. Just as his mother had said, things always turned out well for Eddie Trudeau.

He was working too hard, but so were the other young physicians. He thought that the sudden change from country to city living was responsible for part of the new weariness. Also, getting started in a practice was difficult, and clinic teaching strenuous. He had a slight fever at times but passed it off as due to malaria—a complaint so common even in the city that no one thought much about it. Eventually it would wear itself out.

Luis Walton brought up the subject of this weariness on several occasions when Eddie was too tired to share the work at the clinic. Finally Luis said, "Old boy, you look to me like you have a high fever." Looking at his friend with a critical eye, he added, "You're thin. Even those new side whiskers fail to hide that fact. Your eyes have an unnatural brightness."

Eddie turned away impatiently. "It's nothing—just that malaria. I'll take a dose of quinine. Come on, let's get out of here. Now, that woman with the involvement at the base of her left lung . . ."

"Stop trying to change the subject!" Luis was insistent. "Let me take your temperature." He looked very stern as he shoved the thermometer between Eddie's lips. "Keep your mouth shut!" he said as Eddie tried to protest.

When Walton took the thermometer out and peered at the slim glass tube, he frowned slightly, then walked to the window and looked at it again. The frown deepened, and he turned with a look of dismay in his dark eyes. "I say, it's a hundred and one degrees!"

Eddie gasped. "Whew! That malaria is really kicking up."

"Malaria nothing! You know perfectly well—or you should— that you have something more than malaria. You've had a hacking cough for weeks. You're nervous as a cat and you've lost weight."

"Well, I may have lost a pound or two, but the cough comes from too much pipe smoking." Eddie spoke hopefully.

His friend refused to be quieted. "Now look here. I'm going to give you a little of the talk you pass out at the clinic. There's no point in hiding your head in the sand. If you only have malaria— well, fine. But you *must* find out!"

Eddie felt helpless. "How? Do you want to examine me?"

Walton shook his head. "No indeed! Go to see Janeway. We've come to know him fairly well at Bellevue. All the medical men say he's one of the best young diagnosticians in town."

The next afternoon as Eddie was returning from a call on West 14th Street he passed Dr. Janeway's office, and he stopped a moment to consider. Walton was sure to keep after him. "The trouble with us is," he told himself as he pulled the bell knob, "we think about phthisis so much, we imagine everyone with a cough or fever has it. It could be any number of things."

Fortunately Dr. Janeway was free to see him and immediately began his examination. "Take a deep breath, hold it, then say 'one, two, three,' as you exhale," he ordered when Eddie had pulled off his shirt and was seated on a stool. "Ever had pneumonia?"

"No."

"Any pleurisy on your left side?"

"No."

"Night sweats?"

"No."

"How is your appetite?"

"Good." This was getting ridiculous.

"Lost any weight? Have you been coughing?"

On and on the questions went. Dr. Janeway finished with the stethoscope and began to thump Eddie's chest, first on the upper left side, then on the right. It seemed odd, amusing really, to go through this old routine.

When the physician at last finished, he arose and walked to his desk. His long, heavy face with its bulbous nose looked solemn. Eddie asked with forced cheerfulness, "Well, doctor, how was it? All right, I suppose."

Janeway was never a man to mince words or hedge. Looking straight into Trudeau's eyes, he replied slowly, "There is an involvement in the upper two-thirds of your left lung. You have phthisis."

Eddie was stunned. He managed to stammer his thanks and then rushed out the door. He had been all too willing to think Luis Walton was wrong, but he could not question Dr. Janeway. As he stood on the stoop, dazed and bewildered, a queer thought ran through his brain: "I know just how a man at the bar feels when he hears he is going to be hanged next Tuesday!"

He could not fool himself. Creosote, iodine, cod liver oil, cough medicine—these were only palliatives.

He looked up. The sun was shining, but to him the world had suddenly grown dark. The rush and noise of traffic were something apart from him. Two small boys were playing hopscotch on the sidewalk, carefree, laughing, unconcerned as he stepped around them. There was no joy in *his* world. He had consumption—bother with the fancy medical name. Consumption, the fatal disease that had taken his beloved brother. Oh, they might find ways to prolong his life for a while . . . Here he was, just twenty-six years old. He had accomplished so little.

"Strange," he mused as he hailed a cab, "I never thought it could happen to me!" Did everyone feel that way? As if he of all people led a charmed life?

"Take me to Fifth and Forty-six Street." How could he tell Lottie? He was tempted to change the address, go to the dispensary or talk with Otis first.

He recalled Lottie's bright, happy face as she had kissed him good-by that morning. Only a brief good-by. What about Chatte? And the other baby to be born a few months from now? All his rosy dreams about professional success, all these were gone—gone as suddenly as one blows out a candle. There was no light anywhere. He must tell Lottie at once. They had vowed never to postpone the telling of bad news; they would always be honest with each other—face their troubles as well as their joys together.

He took hold of his own doorknob. Slowly he opened the door and with leaden feet stepped inside.

Lottie's voice filtered down the stairs. "Home so early? I saw you from the window. You walked as if you were very tired. Better take a nap. Oh Eddie, I have such good news! Luis Walton stopped by this morning. He, Al Little and Billy Bull are coming for dinner. Wasn't it jolly of those boys to invite themselves?"

VII.

THE WANDERER

Lottie heard the news without flinching, and her calm acceptance of what she well understood was a most uncertain future for the entire family helped steady her husband's shock and worry. She suggested that they postpone the dinner party for a few days, but he would not hear of it. He had a hunch that his friends had put their heads together and would come up with a plan of some sort.

He was right. As soon as the meal was over and the group was seated in front of the open hearth in the parlor, Luis Walton said, "I talked with Janeway after you saw him, Eddie. I say, his view of your prospects is not completely black."

The sick man's hopes rose. "Just what do you mean by that?"

"People with phthisis have managed to live for many years. Janeway thinks your chances are good if you get out of this rough climate—go to a warm place, say to Aiken, South Carolina."

Bull spoke. "The main point is that you must not lose your strength and appetite. You'll feel more like getting around down there in the sun. Flint says that patients make a mistake by giving way to loss of appetite. You scarcely touched that steak tonight."

Trudeau felt like protesting that after what he had heard today he could not be expected to have a big appetite.

"If you stay out of doors and keep active you will *want* to eat. That's Janeway's theory," Walton said.

Trudeau exchanged glances with Lottie. Her face was composed, her eyes cheerful. How could she, with another baby on the way, with disaster staring at them, be so calm?

Again Walton spoke. "I think that you people should leave at once. Janeway will give you the name of a medical man in Aiken. How does that sound, old boy?"

"I—well—what do you think of all this, Lottie?" Trudeau felt weary and listless, more like just sitting than trying to decide whether he should take a long train journey to a strange place.

"I think we should try, at least. If the doctors advise a warm climate, let us go at once," his wife said in a tone of voice that left no question.

The Trudeaus left two days later for South Carolina, expecting to stay until late spring, but after a month of the regime—daily horseback rides, long walks and futile attempts to eat hearty meals— Trudeau was sicker than when he left New York. He had lost both strength and weight, the exercise left him feverish and he felt tired even in the morning. The sight of his long, thin face in the shaving mirror made him shudder.

It was actually a relief to get back to the blustery spring weather in New York. At least he had an excuse to stay in bed even though he slept only fitfully, night or day.

The chief distress he felt, however, came from the insistence of the doctors on examining him, one after another. Flint, Otis, then Janeway thumped his chest and shook their heads mournfully. Janeway looked especially worried. "Perhaps a mountain climate would agree with you. The change might calm your nerves. I think that New York only makes you more restless, especially since all your friends are working. Have you ever been to the mountains of western North Carolina? Some of my patients found that area beneficial."

Trudeau had no desire to travel South again. It would be the same old story. But Janeway's idea that he leave New York and go to the mountains recalled his wonderful vacation in the Adirondacks, and he spoke about it, telling what the two weeks up there at Paul Smith's had done for him.

The physician agreed that it might be a good idea to go there again, although he doubted that the climate was good for consumptives. So it was decided that he should at least consider it.

The main difficulty was that Lottie was expecting her baby in a few weeks, and Trudeau would not consider leaving until it arrived and Lottie recovered her strength. Naturally he wanted to take his family with him, but Luis Walton counseled against this because of the distance and the difficulty of traveling with a small infant.

"I'll help Lottie and the children move to Douglaston and find someone to take over the lease on this house," he said. "You try the summer up there at St. Regis without the family. You have nothing to worry about here. I'll go out to Douglaston every week end and send reports on the youngsters. Your friend Lou Livingston says he will go up there with you."

With this assurance from Luis, Trudeau felt that he could make no objection to going without his wife and children, and when Lottie herself pronounced it a splendid arrangement, he agreed to go with Lou as his escort.

The baby Edward, whom they called Ned, was born on May 18, 1875, and only a week later Trudeau said a tearful good-by to his wife and children and left the house wondering when, if ever, he would see his little family again. He felt almost as mournful as he had the day he heard that he had consumption.

Lou Livingston bundled him hastily into a waiting cab and they started for the railroad station on the first leg of the tedious journey to St. Regis. "Now calm yourself, fellow, everything is going to be all right. I'll stay for a month at Regis, then Mother will get someone else to come up and keep you company. You'll be perfectly fit in no time," Lou said with what was evidently forced cheerfulness.

Trudeau never had felt less cheerful in his life; still, as he thought about the old hotel and the good times he had had there, his spirits rose a little. "I would rather spend what is left of my life at Uncle

Paul's than lie around here and watch everyone else practice."

"It isn't that bad! Now settle back and leave everything to me."

Mrs. Livingston was waiting at the 42nd Street Station when they arrived a few minutes later. She suggested that they travel only as far as Saratoga on the first day and go by train to Whitehall the next morning for another rest.

Trudeau thought her plan was excellent and when he went aboard the boat at Whitehall for a ride across Lake Champlain on the next leg of their trip, he was feeling less tired than when he left home. But in spite of the clear fresh air and the beautiful scenery, he was quite sick when they pulled up at the dock at Plattsburgh around suppertime. He had a raging fever and was unable to eat anything. He immediately crawled into bed at the Fouquet House. The next morning he was still too ill and weak to try the last part of the trip. When after another day he felt no better, Lou suggested that they stay there for a week. "Or would you rather turn back?"

Trudeau was shocked by this unexpected suggestion. He could not live long if he returned to New York, and the thought of staying in the parsonage with the Reverend Beare and his petty troubles made him groan. "No! What good would that do?"

"Well," Lou hesitated and looked away, "to be perfectly frank, the men downstairs say it's crazy to haul a sick man like you all that distance over such rough roads. You really think you're up to it?"

"Give me one more day and I will be." Somehow he must manage to travel the rest of the distance, rough roads or no.

The next morning they boarded the branch railroad train and rode to Ausable Forks. While Trudeau rested in the station Lou went in search of a livery stable. He returned all smiles to say that he had hired a man with a two-horse stage wagon to drive the forty miles to St. Regis. "I fastened a board between the back seats, borrowed a mattress and pillows and blankets, so you'll be able to lie down all the way."

Trudeau lay on this crude bed as the horses plodded up the hills and trotted down again. It was difficult to say which was the harder to bear—going up or going down. Either way he had to hold tight to keep from rolling onto the floor. He lay there clutching the mattress and boards, listening to Lou and the driver as they smoked and told silly stories, apparently quite comfortable and contented with the slow pace. When Lou turned to ask how he was doing, Trudeau pretended to be asleep. He could not tell the truth and spoil their fun. It was not Lou's fault that the road was rough, the bed hard.

The trip seemed endless. Even on the level the corduroy road almost shook his teeth loose. At several points he thought of asking them to find a farmhouse where they could stay overnight, but this would complicate matters, making it necessary for the driver to spend an extra night on the road and increasing the expense. On and on they rode. It was sunset when at last they reached the turn into Paul Smith's.

"Hooray! We're here!" Lou shouted.

Trudeau sat up. Through the grove of pines he saw the hotel, the peaceful lake out beyond. Someone called, "Here they come!"

By the time the wagon pulled up to the horse-block a dozen or so guides and sportsmen were rushing out to greet them. Fred Martin led the pack. As he lunged forward with hand outstretched, Trudeau winced. In his present condition Martin's handshake would crush his bones. He kept his arms under the blanket and said, with as much strength as he could muster, "I'm sick." All his strength was gone and his bones ached from lying on the hard wagon all day. Glad though he was to be here, he could not move to get out of the makeshift bed. "I'm sick," he repeated.

Martin leaned over him, as if to hear more clearly. His smile faded. "Tarnation! I believe you are sick!"

"Could you carry me up to my room?" The words came in a half-whisper while the others crowded around, peering over Martin's shoulder.

Without another word the guide picked him up as if he were a sack of sugar and mounted the steps, kicked the door open, crossed the parlor and bounded up the two flights, two steps at a time. Then he gently laid Trudeau on the wide bed and said in a pained and sorrowful tone, "Why, doctor, you don't weigh no more than a dried lambskin!"

Exhausted though he was, Trudeau had to smile.

A few minutes later Paul and his wife came in. "We just got back from town," the hotelkeeper said. "Sorry we weren't the first to greet you." The Smiths stood at the foot of the bed, their faces wearing forced smiles.

"This is a far cry from my first arrival at your hotel, isn't it?" Trudeau asked.

"Poor boy!" Mrs. Smith said, shaking her head. "But I'm glad you wanted to come to us."

Paul seemed to have recovered from his shock. "Yes indeed. There is no one I would rather have to usher in the season! Brace up. What you need is to be away from those old sawbones."

Mrs. Smith nudged her husband. "You forget he's now *Doctor* Trudeau."

"Well, so he is. I'll overlook that though."

"Come, Paul, let the doctor rest up for dinner."

As Trudeau lay on the comfortable bed and breathed the clean, invigorating air, his muscles gradually relaxed and he became drowsy. He was about to fall asleep when Paul entered the room with a kerosene lamp in one hand, a tray balanced on the other arm. "Just smell this, young man!"

Trudeau sat up. There was enough food on the tray to feed two hungry woodsmen—lake trout, scrambled eggs, pancakes and coffee. "Do you think I can eat all that?"

"See that you do. Mama might scold if you send any of it back. She caught that fish herself this afternoon."

Trudeau knew perfectly well that Mrs. Smith had no time for the luxury of fishing, but he said nothing and began to eat. To his surprise, he was able to consume every scrap of the delicious food. When Mrs. Smith brought another cup of coffee he confessed, "That is the most I have eaten since the Livingstons and I were here the first time."

A few minutes later Trudeau again lay back on the thick pillows of his warm bed, listening to the wind as it whistled through the white curtains. Soon he fell asleep and did not waken until morning, when he heard the hounds baying, eager for the trail. His

thoughts turned to Lottie, Chatte, the baby Ned and the early-
morning bustle in the small house on 46th Street. Luis Walton
would arrive during the day to take them to Douglaston. If friends
could help, certainly his were doing all they could . . . He thought
about the clinic—that poor, thin Mrs. Calahan would be in today,
as she was every Thursday. She had brought a little bouquet of
flowers when she first heard of his illness. So sick, yet she thought
only of others. These were the cases that warmed a physician's
heart—the grateful, the uncomplaining, who did exactly as they
were told. But he must not think about these things.

After he had eaten a large breakfast Warren Flanders, his old
guide, came into the room. "I see you slicked the tray, doctor. You
need a full belly because we're going hunting!"

Trudeau sighed and shook his head. "I couldn't walk downstairs,
let alone through the first carry."

Flanders raised his big hands. "Hold your horses. There's no call
for you to walk at all. We can spot game right from my boat. I fixed
it up real comfortable with balsam boughs and blankets. Your rifle
is cleaned and ready. You'll be a lot better off than in that old bed.
You don't have to lift a finger, if you've no mind to. I will row
downriver, kind of slow, to Keese's Mill and we'll see what we can
see. How about it?"

The guide looked so hopeful, so determined, that Trudeau did
not have the nerve to say no. "All right, I'll try!" he said as he
swung his feet over the side of the bed.

It was a beautiful sunny day, warm and friendly. The wind was
down and the sky and water a deep sapphire blue. Trudeau lay on
the boughs in the stern of the boat, his rifle across the gunwale.
Strangely, he did feel better, and the prospect of hunting even in
this ludicrous fashion aroused his love of the sport. As Flanders
expertly skimmed the water with his oars, pulling the boat gently
across the broad expanse of Lower St. Regis and into the river,
Trudeau marveled at the beauty of the new foliage, the quiet, the
warmth of the sun as it touched his face and filtered through the
blanket. June was wonderful in this mountain country, so full of
promise. He could not possibly think of misery and sickness. All

memory of troubles in the past two months melted away.

When they entered the river he noticed that Flanders kept looking ahead and stopping frequently to peer through the trees. He paddled on to a wide spot where there was a large cluster of water-lily plants, then stopped again and turned the boat sidewise as he motioned with his head.

On a point of land not two hundred yards distant were two deer feeding—a five-point buck and a doe. The buck raised his head and stretched his long, graceful neck.

A thrill ran through Trudeau as his right hand slipped forward and grasped the butt of his rifle. He turned it quietly on the gunwale and took aim without even sitting up. He fired. The buck jumped several times, then went down at the edge of the woods with a loud thud while the doe bounded away among the trees and brush.

A deep sense of contentment flowed through Trudeau's veins. What a sight those animals were! That a wonderful buck! He laid his rifle beside him and settled back to rest his head on the pillows as Flanders waded ashore.

"I think you got him right through the neck," Flanders said. In a short time he dragged the heavy animal to the shore, pulled up the boat, dressed the buck, and loaded it. "What do you say we go back now? I can't wait to brag on this one!"

Trudeau smiled wryly, trying to appear modest. "Better not brag too much. That was just luck."

"Luck, nothin'! Nobody but you could-a done that flat on his back! Sometimes I think your aim is best when you don't stop to figure. Just the opposite with most folks."

Trudeau smiled happily as Flanders rowed swiftly across the lake toward the hotel, talking all the time in his low, drawling voice. When they reached the landing, Trudeau stepped out and walked to the veranda without help.

He slept all afternoon. As he lay in his bed that night, looking out of the window at the full moon and the gently swaying pines, he was happy. Had he really done a foolish thing, coming to St. Regis? For some reason, all he had learned about phthisis ran through his mind. He wondered if Frank might have lived longer up here in these quiet, clean woods. Certainly that stuffy, overheated room with its windows tightly closed did not help. Was he imagining things? It would be silly to draw conclusions from the experience of a single day. Most unscientific, as Dr. Clark would say. Still, he did feel better already. There was something about these north woods . . .

He forgot to take his temperature that night, and from then on the thermometer Luis had given him lay unused on his dresser. Every morning, except when it rained or there was a high wind, he went out in the boat with Flanders or Lou, and in the afternoon stretched out for a long nap on the couch that Mrs. Smith placed on the back porch for him, where he would not be disturbed by guests coming and going. The weeks passed quickly. He was sure that he was gaining weight, and little by little the cough had quieted. At the end of July, Lou Livingston bade him good-by with tears in his eyes. "Ed will be here tomorrow, fellow."

It was unlike Lou to be so emotional.

Ed Harriman came with good news from Lottie. The children were thriving and she insisted on sending an apple cake baked for him by Eliza. "Infernal nuisance, but I had to humor them."

Luis Walton had faithfully sent weekly reports, all good, but it was more reassuring to receive news of his family, firsthand.

"That boy of yours is handsome. Doesn't look a bit like you, except for his pointed chin. Got his mother's head, thank heavens. No bulging dome," Ed said, apparently unaware that he was presenting Trudeau with a barbed compliment.

When Ed left two weeks later he, too, had tears in his eyes.

"What *is* this?" Trudeau asked of Uncle Paul when his friend had gone.

The hotel man cleared his throat. "To be truthful, I am under the impression they think they are saying good-by for good. I don't agree, of course. My motto is, keep your feet warm, your head cool, and stay away from doctors if you want to be healthy. Always worked for me. And I don't give a continental what that Livingston or Harriman thinks: you *are* better."

Then Jim Livingston came for three weeks. At the end of his visit Trudeau felt so well that he decided to go back with him as far as

Catskill, New York, where Lottie, her father and the children were vacationing. He was tanned, fifteen pounds heavier, his cough had gone and he was sure that his fever had too, although the thermometer was still in its case.

The reunion was wonderful, of course. Trudeau was delighted to see that Chatte was beginning to walk and that Ned was indeed handsome, with large, intelligent eyes. He was not a fat baby but he looked healthy. They stayed on for several days, then went to Douglaston. Trudeau enjoyed being with his family so much that he dreaded to leave them long enough to go into New York to see Dr. Janeway. Finally Luis insisted that he make an appointment.

"When can I begin my practice?" he asked when the examination was over.

Janeway looked surprised. "Not until and not unless I say so. Phthisis has a way of coming back. You know that. Your chest is quiet now. Better be satisfied just to hold your own. Half a loaf is better than none. If you're careful you could live for years."

Trudeau was grateful for this stern, though realistic, reminder and he resolved to do his best to be happy, merely to live comfortably with his family. But after only two weeks his fever and cough returned and again he lost his appetite.

This time Janeway suggested that he try the sunny winter of Minnesota where, according to the latest reports, a number of consumptives had benefited. The treatment was to be the same—driving, walking and duck hunting on good days.

With some misgivings Trudeau took his family to Minnesota. He followed Janeway's instructions, although the activity usually left him exhausted and with a high fever. By spring he was as sick as before, so they left St. Paul in June. He was determined to go back to the Adirondacks—and with his family. After only a few days at Douglaston, off they went by train—Lottie, the children, one nurse and Eddie—bound for Paul Smith's and the north woods.

This time it was the children who responded immediately to the wild, wonderful country. Trudeau gained strength very slowly. He had no desire to hunt, even by boat, and refused all the guides' ingenious coaxing.

Fortunately a physician arrived at St. Regis in September, Dr. Alfred Loomis, a man of slight build, with dark eyes and hair and a ruddy complexion typical of one who spends much time out of doors.

Loomis, born in Bennington, Vermont, in 1831, had lost both of his parents from tuberculosis while he was only a child. Although short of funds, he had managed to secure a college education and later was graduated from the College of Physicians and Surgeons, a superior student who was expected to go far. Loomis soon discovered that he had a mild case of tuberculosis, and since heavy exercise was the prescribed rule in 1862, he spent as much time as he could spare from his large practice hunting and fishing in the Adirondacks. By the time Trudeau met him in 1875 he seemed to be fairly well, and now had a reputation as a leading student of phthisis and clinical teacher in New York City. He came with a party of sportsmen for a month of camping and hunting and agreed, on Paul's invitation, to stop in on his return to examine Trudeau.

Loomis gave him a thorough examination. "I'm afraid that I cannot be very encouraging. What are your plans for the winter— not New York, I hope? The temptation to plunge into work is too great down there."

Trudeau could not argue about this, although work was far from a temptation to him now. It was the idea of moving to a new place, no matter how quiet, that wearied him. "To be truthful, I'm tired to death of chasing around from here to there. What I would like best is to stay right here at Paul's."

Dr. Loomis cocked one eyebrow. "This hotel closes the end of the month, you know."

"Yes, I know." The Smiths themselves would stay on through the long winter with a man to take care of the horses and barn and a woman to help with the cooking and cleaning.

"If you really are intent on staying up here, I don't think it would harm you, exactly. You might as well live where you are happiest. It could prolong your life," Dr. Loomis said. He was a smallish man, quiet-spoken yet positive. He stroked his walrus moustache thoughtfully as he talked. "My patient, Mr. Edgar, expects to stay over at Saranac Lake this winter. He will be at Martin's Hotel. You might think about that."

Trudeau still had a horror of moving, even the fourteen miles to Saranac Lake—a place he had not seen. He was determined to see what he could do with Paul Smith.

The hotel man at first refused to talk about keeping the Trudeaus through the winter. There would be no doctor for the children. What if one of them took sick?

"Well, I'm a doctor—or *was*," Trudeau argued.

"What about yourself?"

Trudeau eyed Paul narrowly. "I seem to recall that you think people should keep away from doctors."

Paul smiled at this reminder. "Well, talk it over with Mama."

From the first it had been evident that Lottie and Mrs. Smith liked each other, and all summer the two women had spent the evenings sewing, talking about their children, exchanging recipes and indulging in all kinds of woman-talk. It would be best to ask Lottie to persuade Mrs. Smith.

Just as Trudeau expected, Lottie did.

VIII.

SNOWBOUND

The last of the summer guests left Paul Smith's in October. By early November all the other hotels and camps in the north woods were boarded up for the winter, and the Trudeaus settled themselves for a long, quiet stay at St. Regis. The mere prospect of remaining there lifted the sick man's spirit. The improvement in his health, so long delayed this time, came slowly. He knew that he was better several weeks before anyone but Lottie noticed it. By mid-November his fever had subsided, he was gaining weight and coughed only in the morning, although he was still short of breath and could walk only as far as the barn without stopping for a rest. Even so, he was able to do a little hunting. Large white rabbits were plentiful near the hotel and Trudeau enjoyed sitting on a stump to take aim at them as they hopped across the snowy slopes.

"There is an old saying," Paul Smith observed one evening when they were seated in front of the fireplace in the Trudeaus' room, "that the more you walk the less you hunt. And it is true. People would do better if they stayed put on the trails, where the guides tell them to stand. That makes for more sport and better results. But the green ones will not listen. They are in too much of a hurry."

"Patience is hard to learn for some people," Lottie said, "but my husband is learning it."

Patience on the trail, patience in fighting consumption . . . yes, that was what he must strive for, Trudeau thought as he sat holding the sleeping baby Ned and watching Chatte squatted on the floor surrounded by her wooden blocks. In the past fifteen minutes she had laboriously set up her tower, only to have it topple at least a dozen times. She would continue to build until the blocks remained as she wanted them. She always did. His daughter was patient—just like her mother—he told himself with a sigh. Chatte looked like her Grandfather Berger, round-faced, bright, dark eyes.

Lottie and the Smiths were playing whist when Paul suddenly dropped his cards with a bang on the table, reached in his vest pocket and pulled out a small blue envelope. "Oh, forgive me, doctor, I forgot to give you this."

"Why, Paul Smith," his wife said, "it came yesterday. Brink brought it in with the supplies from Malone!"

Trudeau was too pleased to see his mother's handwriting to be provoked with his friend. Her weekly letters seldom had any exciting news. Usually they told of her quiet life in Fontainebleau or a trip she and her husband were planning to Italy or Switzerland, but they always reflected her zest for life, her deep interest in her son and his family. Trudeau had written her only the bare details of his illness, so he was surprised to read, "I am deeply worried about you. I can stand it no longer. Let me know how to reach that wilderness, and I will take the next steamer for America."

The Smiths appeared worried when he read this part of the letter to them. An elderly lady coming in winter to St. Regis?

Lottie quieted their fears. "Oh, Madame Chuffart will love it here. She's so lively. Eddie, that's wonderful news. Now, suppose we do this . . ." she said as she collected the cards.

Lottie and the children would go down to Little Neck to visit her father and secure another nursemaid to assist Ann Gaffney, the regular one, so that Lottie would be free to spend more time with him on her return. Trudeau and his mother could have a long visit and talk to their hearts' content. When Madame Chuffart had to leave they would all meet somewhere for a day or two, so the children could get acquainted with their grandmother. They could put her on the train, then come back with Trudeau to Uncle Paul's.

"It sounds like a good plan," Mrs. Smith agreed. "I only hope we're not snowbound when that time comes."

The next month was a long one for Trudeau, especially the last few days after Lottie and the children left for New York, but the weather was clear and unusually warm for early December. On the day Fred Martin drove to Ausable Forks to meet the train, Trudeau was too excited even to shoot rabbits. The day seemed endless to him, but at sundown the Smiths' two older boys, Phelps and Paul, who had posted themselves on a hilltop behind the house to signal the arrival of the cutter, came whooping down the slope.

"They're here! Here they come!"

Trudeau ran out to the horse-block to greet his mother who hopped out of the cutter, all smiles. "Why, Eddie! You look better than you did when you were in Paris!" She hugged him close and looked up at his face. "And what have you done? Your face looks wider somehow."

Eddie laughed. He was too excited and happy to speak.

His mother clapped her white-gloved hands. "I know, you have grown mutton-chop whiskers!"

They walked arm in arm up the steps. Madame Chuffart was bubbling over with talk. The trip was beautiful, she was not at all tired, it was like a miracle to see him, how was Lottie? Where was she? How about Chatte and Ned?

When they went inside, Trudeau was amused to see how Mrs. Smith, Paul and the guides gathered around his mother, obviously delighted. He knew that they had all dreaded the arrival of this "French" lady, but here they were, falling over one another in their eagerness to take her wraps, carry her bags, see her to her room and make sure that she was not overtired. Paul rushed to the kitchen and returned with a tray bearing the old gallon coffee pot.

"Oh Paul!" his wife exclaimed, "I polished the silver urn. Take that awful tin thing right back!"

Madame Chuffart darted across the room. "Why, he must not! My son promised to show me how things are done in the north woods. Pouring from this pot will be my first lesson!"

Paul Smith beamed. "Like mother, like son. I can see right now that you are exactly alike!"

Trudeau put his arm around his mother. "Well, except that my nose is straighter and I am about twice her height!"

For the first few days he scarcely had a chance to visit alone with his mother. When she was not telling amusing stories about her travels, Paul spun yarns about the early days in the Adirondacks or someone suggested that they play whist. When mother and son at last talked themselves out, there were many other things to do. Madame wanted to see the woods and mountains, to ride on the frozen lake in the sleigh and on sunny days to play in the snow with the Smith boys. Trudeau even taught her to shoot—and she was remarkably good at it.

Suddenly he noticed that he was no longer tired in the mornings; even after a walk, if he did not go too far, he returned refreshed, eager to eat a large breakfast, then visit before the fire. During these weeks he settled into a pleasant routine—moderate exercise, rest in the afternoon and talk or whist in the evenings. His mother had brought her paints and sketch pads along and insisted on giving him a few art lessons. "Of course, you can learn," she insisted with motherly pride. "I am a pretty fair artist, and as you know, your father has done beautiful things!"

Trudeau turned out an oil showing a large white rabbit, quite unlike any ever seen at St. Regis, but his mother thought it was lovely. "All you need is practice and patience, son."

Patience again! He shook his head. "Painting doesn't mean enough to me for that."

The weeks passed quickly. Everyone agreed that Madame Chuffart's visit had served as a wonderful diversion, for she had brought new topics, a shift of interest which before had settled on her son. Now everything revolved around his mother, even his own thoughts. When in mid-January she announced that she must leave for a visit with Adelina, Paul begged her to remain a few weeks longer. No, her mind was made up.

There was no sense in arguing. Trudeau knew that there was a bit of Granny's stubbornness in his mother.

The weather was fine the day mother and son set off in the sleigh drawn by a little mare he had purchased some time earlier. They were to meet Lottie, the two nursemaids and the children at Malone, forty miles distant. As they passed through the snow-covered woods, by frozen lakes and through wild, open stretches with houses usually six to ten miles apart, Trudeau wondered that Paul had allowed him to start off on this trip. "It must be that he thinks I can manage, no matter what," he told himself as the mare stumbled along the unbroken road. His mother was evidently unaware of any danger— the possibility that the sleigh might upset in a snowdrift—for she exclaimed over the beauty of the country, how much fun the visit had been, and said that it would now be easier to bear the separation.

They reached Malone at dusk.

Two days later, after a pleasant family reunion, the Trudeaus went to the station to see Madame Chuffart begin her train journey. Her only tears came with her final good-by to him. "I cannot bear to lose another son."

Then Paul Smith arrived with a sleigh to carry the Trudeaus and Ann Gaffney and Mary Smith, the two nurses, back to St. Regis. He also had a lumber sled, pulled by two large horses and driven by the teamster Brink, to carry the trunks and bags.

It was snowing a little when they started the next morning, but Trudeau was so pleased to have his family with him again, and so eager to get back to the hotel, that he gave no thought to the possibility of a heavy storm. Paul rode with Brink on the sled, the nurses and children in one sleigh, Trudeau and Lottie in the other. There was much singing and calling back and forth when they began the slow ascents, but as the wind rose and it grew colder, everyone quieted. Lottie talked about her father, about a few of Trudeau's patients at Douglaston, of Luis Walton and his other medical friends who had come out to the parsonage to visit her. Several times Trudeau was on the verge of asking questions about his former patients, but a strange feeling that all this was part of the dim past came over him. New York and Long Island seemed far, far away.

"You know, Lottie, I'm actually learning to take Janeway's advice seriously. It's better to be content with half a loaf. I'm lucky just to be alive, to have you and the children with me. I must not think about the future."

"It's better that way," Lottie said as she pulled up the bearskin rug to shield her eyes from the powdery snow.

There were drifts across the road now, concealing the path made by the horses and sleighs the night before. Frequently the snow was so deep that Eddie and Lottie had to walk long distances, while the nurses separated, obviously frightened now, each took a child with her to ride in the sleighs. It was hard to say which was harder to bear—going through the open hollows where there was nothing to stop the drifts or riding through the forested areas where the wind howled mournfully in the trees. It was getting much colder and they could see only a short distance ahead. Ned and Chatte started to cry. Twice each sleigh overturned, dumping the screaming nurses and children into the drifts. Then Trudeau and Paul had to run back to put everything to rights.

Finally Paul came over to talk with the Trudeaus. "I just examined that hill ahead. It is solid with snow. I am afraid it will take a while to dig our way through, and the children might freeze to death. We must get some kind of shelter."

Trudeau looked around. "Is there a farmhouse near?"

"Not very. I'll ask Brink to help dig a big hole in this drift. You crawl in while we unharness the horses and try to break through."

Lottie went to quiet Ned in the lead-sleigh. Trudeau, listening to the dismal wails of the children, was now thoroughly alarmed. While he blanketed the horses, the other two men dug a giant hole into the drift on the lee side of the hill. When the bearskin robes were placed inside and everyone crouched together away from the bitter cold, the youngsters quieted at last and he felt better.

"Why, it is quite comfortable in here," Lottie said.

For the moment, at least, they were safe.

After a short crying spell the nurse Mary looked at Trudeau. "I don't see why I left New York!" Again she burst into tears.

It was several hours later when Paul succeeded in completing a trail. Then everyone piled in again and rode to the top of the hill, where the hotelman harnessed his large horses to one sleigh. Into this piled the Trudeaus and the nurses. Brink rode one of the draft horses harnessed to the sled, while Paul piloted the mare and empty sleigh himself. At last Trudeau saw a glimmer of light through the trees. Paul announced, "Duanes' farm!"

"Thank goodness!" Those were the first words Lottie had spoken since they had left their dugout.

Soon they were inside the house, warming their hands before a blazing fire. The children danced around to thaw their feet, then all sat down to supper.

"I think this is a beautiful house," Trudeau said. How lucky they had been to reach it.

His wife nodded. "And the food is delicious."

Mr. and Mrs. Duane smiled.

The next morning dawned clear and cold. Paul said that the thermometer read 20 degrees below zero. "I'll go ahead to check the condition of the road. It would be silly for you folks to leave this warm house just yet."

Nurse Ann Gaffney said, "As far as I am concerned, I would just as soon stay here until spring!"

Everyone but the new nurse laughed at this. She shook her head. "All I ask is to live until I get back to the city!"

Paul Smith frowned. "I think you can manage to do that. Now you folks stay here today while Brink and I make our trail to the next farm and get a fresh team. It's only about ten miles. We'll dig out the worst of the drifts, then take you through tomorrow, early."

They were still nearly twenty-eight miles from the hotel. The first ten led through the woods, Paul said.

When they resumed their journey the following day, progress was slow but not difficult until they reached the open road where they found new drifts. They drew up to the McCollums' farm, only seven miles from the hotel, in early afternoon. Again Paul suggested that he and Brink go ahead to break trail. After a good meal at McCollum's, including an extra hour of rest for the horses, the two sleighs started. Paul and Brink had checked ahead for only a short distance and had decided that they would have no further trouble. A short time later they saw new drifts, which had developed during the day. The going was extremely heavy now, especially when they tried to cross a wide, burned-over area with snow as much as six feet deep. They had to stop a number of times. The Trudeaus tried to comfort the children and nurses while the men dug. Unfortunately there were no landmarks here, no sign of the actual road, and the hollows were entirely filled, so that again the sleighs upset.

The smaller horses were covered with frozen sweat and could scarcely walk, let alone drag the sleighs. When Paul came back to talk with him in late afternoon, Trudeau could see that he was worried. "We might as well leave the trunks and bags, and harness the heavy team to this sleigh. Come back tomorrow for the stuff."

"How much farther is it?" Lottie asked.

"About three miles. We're near Barnum Pond."

It was snowing hard again and night was coming on. Trudeau looked at Paul in his big buffalo coat with its red woolen sash around the middle. It was a great comfort to have this capable, seasoned woodsman remain calm and self-assured. He would manage to get them through safely.

Reaching the slope above Barnum Pond, the two big draft horses suddenly stopped and lay down on their sides in the snow.

Trudeau did not want to voice his thoughts. They could not stay here all night; yet with the two small horses almost worn out too, how could they go on? These animals certainly could not break trail.

"Doctor," Paul said as they all stood gazing at the large horses lying in the snow, "I seem to remember Napoleon said that the dark regions of Russia are fit only for the Russians. Your missus is going to think the same thing about the north woods."

Trudeau was in no mood to appreciate a joke. "What are you going to do?"

"We will have to go on foot."

"And leave the horses to die?" Lottie asked.

This time Trudeau did feel like laughing. His wife was in mortal danger, and still she could think about the horses!

"Oh, they'll get up when they're rested." Paul turned around. "Lant Wilcox lives half a mile from here. You folks wait. I'll go and get a fresh team. Brink will look after ours. Keep as warm as you can until I get back. It won't take long."

When he finally returned with the fresh team harnessed to a lumber sled, everyone climbed on. Paul shook the reins, and at ten o'clock they drew up in front of the hotel. Paul's own team and the mares were dragging but still alive, far to the rear.

The hotel had never looked so beautiful to Eddie. He and everyone else were worn out and ravenously hungry. Mrs. Smith stirred up the fires and warmed the supper. Trudeau went to bed as soon as he had eaten, weary but with none of the aching exhaustion that came from fever. He felt surprisingly well, he told Lottie, considering the awful ordeal.

The following morning he and Brink took the lumber sled down to Barnum Pond to rescue the trunks and Paul's sled, almost buried in snow. As they drove up to the spot—or as near as they could get to it—Brink pointed to a depression in the snow. "See there!"

Not twenty feet from where they had stood waiting for Paul in the darkness was a deep, wide hole! Trudeau looked at Brink and knew that his own face must reflect the same mixture of horror and relief. Many times during the arduous trip they had been close to disaster, but never closer than when they stopped here, only three miles from their destination . . .

Trudeau found Lottie sitting by the fire, her Bible unopened in her lap. Had she prayed during the storm? Of course, she must have.

It had not occurred to him to pray, but now, as he walked to the window and looked out at the snow-covered ground, at the pine boughs dragging under the weight of thick white garlands, at the small clearing near the top of the hill where the vegetable garden lay blanketed, Frank's favorite prayer came to him—not a prayer as some would call it, but a Psalm. He could not recall all of it, but some of the words he would never forget:

> *He that dwelleth in the secret place of the Most High shall abide under the shadow of the Almighty. I will say of the Lord, He is my refuge and my fortress; My God, in him will I trust.*

He spoke aloud, and when he finished, Lottie said, "Psalm ninety-one. I think the ninety-second Psalm is even more appropriate."

"I don't remember it. How does it go?"

Lottie smiled and repeated softly: " *'It is a good thing to give thanks unto the Lord, And to sing praises unto thy name, O most High; To show forth thy loving-kindness in the morning, and thy faithfulness every night.'* "

They were both silent for a time, then Lottie spoke again. "You know, I feared more for you than for the rest of us. The children kept warm by crying and fighting the cold. Are you sure that you are all right?"

Trudeau turned from the window. Lottie's face was soft and beautiful in the reflected firelight. She was not beautiful really— not as a man usually thinks of beauty. Her nose was a little irregular, her chin too strong, but she had serenity and dignity of spirit, beauty of character, which shone in her blue eyes.

He sat beside her on the small sofa and took her hand in his. "Lottie, with your help, with your faith and strength, I will keep on top of this trouble of mine. But I need this place, these woods, the peace of the north country."

"I know that you do."

"You, the woods and faith. These I must have—and patience. Isn't there something in one Psalm about 'my springs are in Thee'?"

Lottie shook her head as she did when she scolded Chatte or Ned. "It is a good thing that Father is not here. He would make you study your Catechism all over again."

Paul came to the door to announce dinner. "I see you are both thawed out—none the worse, I take it. Do you want to give this country back to the bears?"

"No. Lottie and I are going to ask the bears to move over. There should be room for all of us here—bears, deer, fox and rabbits. We are in the Adirondacks to stay!"

IX.

THE SEARCH FOR A HOME

The rest of the winter of 1875-76 passed more slowly. After the excitement of Madam Chuffart's visit and the narrow escape from disaster, everyone was glad to settle into a quiet routine, although nurse Mary was obviously unhappy. Several more heavy snowstorms forced Trudeau to give up even short hunting trips, and the men discontinued the twice-weekly trips in the cutter for supplies. Trudeau missed these chances to see new faces. He contented himself with learning the Morse code, and within a short time was able to hold evening talks with the Plattsburg operator across the wire which usually remained closed after the last guests left the hotel in October. Everyone enjoyed this brief daily contact with the outside world. It was just enough to keep them from feeling isolated.

During this period Trudeau continued to gain strength and weight, and felt well enough to play games with Chatte and take her sledding near the hotel. It gradually dawned on him that there might be some connection between the enforced idleness of the closed winter and the course of his disease. He could not attribute his better health entirely to climate. Was rest, then, actually a factor? The idea came slowly, since he was still imbued with the theories taught by his professors and his own physicians: that exercise was essential in the fight against phthisis. His belief in the importance of rest was strengthened when he noticed he did not feel so well during the summer after he resumed his long hunting trips and the hotel filled with interesting guests whose presence gave him little time for long, lazy days. He resolved to speak of his theory to Dr. Loomis when he came up for his autumn hunt.

Alfred L. Loomis, with a large and lucrative practice among wealthy New Yorkers, was generally polished and tactful, but with a fellow physician he could be frank and even blunt. He admitted that he was surprised to find Eddie heavier than he had been the year before and obviously stronger.

"You should have seen me in the spring!"

Loomis shook his head. "Well, I must tell you that your chest findings are about the same as when I first examined you, doctor. No worse, no better: you are holding your own."

Trudeau was disappointed at hearing this, but in the light of his own knowledge he had to admit that he could not expect a miracle. He took the opportunity to tell about his new theory.

Loomis listened politely. "Ordinarily, I would put that down to imagination. We both know that rest as a treatment for consumptives is contrary to our medical teachings. As for myself, I would not run the risk of staying up here in this damp cold, being shut in during long snowstorms, unable to take outdoor exercise for weeks at a time. However, I noticed when Mr. Edgar came to New York last spring for a visit that he had actually improved a little during his winter at Saranac Lake."

"You see!" Trudeau was delighted to hear this. "There must be something in what I say!"

Loomis snapped the lock on his bag and glanced over his shoulder. "Well, I think we might say that this mountain climate compares favorably with that of Minnesota or the Rockies in winter. Your general improvement might have been due to the intense cold, not to enforced idleness. That in itself is something to talk about."

Trudeau was impatient with this reservation. "But I didn't improve one bit in Minnesota! I got worse. I still say that I held my own last winter because I took things easy, and did not chase around."

Loomis shrugged his shoulders and started for the door.

Trudeau felt inclined to argue. "I wish you had examined me in June."

The other doctor was evidently not convinced or willing to pursue the conversation. He said only that he saw no reason why both Trudeau and Mr. Edgar should not try another winter in the Adirondacks. "It goes against the grain to make hasty conclusions about the effects of rest."

Trudeau knew that this was a fair statement. It was difficult to be scientific about your own medical problems, and no good doctor would jump to conclusions from brief experience with one or two patients. He would just have to wait and hope that Loomis would finally come around to his way of thinking.

Since Trudeau had come to associate his chance of prolonging his life and maintaining "a grip on the tiger" with staying at St. Regis, the news that Paul and his wife were leaving in November to take over the management of the Fouquet House at Plattsburg for the winter was a heavy blow. He was only partially mollified by the Smiths' offer to give him the use of a team so that he could drive around the Adirondacks to find another winter residence. The generous friends even offered to loan furniture, bedding and dishes if the Trudeaus decided to rent an unfurnished house.

Lottie took the nurses and children to Douglaston to visit her father while Trudeau searched for a place to live. It was obvious that to Mary, the younger nurse, this was no visit. "Good-by, doctor," she said as they shook hands at the horse-block, "it was nice meeting you." But Ann Gaffney, who had been with Lottie most of the time since Chatte's birth, promised to return.

As Mrs. Smith's brother, Douglas Martin, drove through the mountains with Trudeau, it began to look as if the search was useless. There was nothing in Bloomingdale, nothing in Malone nor in any of a half-dozen villages they visited. Trudeau was now desperate. Lottie had written that she was expecting another baby and was determined to return so she could be with him when the infant arrived in the spring. Under these circumstances they could not very well live at Martin's Hotel in Saranac Lake, where Mr. Edgar was staying. Doug suggested that they go there on the chance of finding an empty house.

"It's not much of a town, of course, but it is old for these parts." The first settler had been Jacob Moody, hunter and trapper. A few years later, in about 1822, an old veteran named Captain Pliny Miller opened a sawmill and a small hotel. It had been a town for guides and lumbermen since that time.

As they drove along the Saranac River, then down into a deep basin with a small lake over to one side, Doug resumed his story. "That's Lake Flower, yonder. Now those frame houses are about all there is to the place, that and the hotel at the intersection. Milo Miller's store is the real hub of Saranac. We'll pull up there and see if Milo can help us."

Trudeau stopped outside the door on the wide boardwalk to look around. Doug was understating things when he said that Saranac Lake was not much of a town. It was only a village with no more than twelve houses. The streets were wide and muddy, one long, winding street crossed by two or three others. The buildings were far apart, as if they had been placed in order to stretch the limits of the town. When Trudeau stepped inside the clapboard building, he found a long, cluttered room with a high ceiling. The counters were wide, the shelves loaded with shoe lacings, shoes, stove polish, tobacco, patent medicines, bolts of calico, overalls, heavy jackets, gloves and other necessities.

Douglas Martin was talking to Mr. Miller, a brisk, overalled man wearing a bright red flannel shirt. The storekeeper stopped talking to look Trudeau up and down with obvious interest. "A doctor, huh? That's good. Old Martin—Doug's kinsman, you know—he owns the hotel. He'll be mighty happy if we get you here in Saranac, Dr. Trudeau."

Trudeau was puzzled by this statement until Mr. Miller explained that the hotel man had to look after the sick. He went on to tell a story about Mr. Martin's little girl who had been taken sick a number of years ago and had nearly died before her father got through the snow to Bloomingdale for help. The girl recovered but her father made up his mind to study medical books. "He goes as far away as ten miles. Only help he gets is from a doctor out of Albany, who comes each fall and spring to hunt."

The thought of people being dependent on an amateur physician made Trudeau shudder, but he was alarmed by the implication that he would immediately assume a heavy country practice. Fortunately, Doug explained that this was not possible in spite of the doctor's apparent good health.

With this point settled, Trudeau waited while Martin and Miller went out to do "a little scouting." While they were gone, a man dressed in hip boots and a heavy mackinaw, a typical woodsman's hat with ear flaps tied over the top of his head, rushed into the store.

"My mother is bilious," he explained to the young clerk who up to the moment had been busy at the telegraph key. "She's got spots in front of her eyes and an awful headache. Can't keep nothing on her stomach. I says to her, 'Ma, you need a round of calomel.' "

The clerk glanced in Trudeau's direction, a question in his eyes. "Who is that?" the customer asked in a low tone.

"That's Dr. Trudeau from Paul Smith's place. He's been to college. What do you say, Doc? Should I sell him liver pills or calomel?"

Trudeau came forward. "Well, I would hate to prescribe either one—offhand. If you want me to, I'll take a look at your mother, sir." When he saw the look of surprise on the clerk's face, he added, "No, I'll make no charge." He completely forgot his vow to keep from practicing medicine.

This was the beginning. Even while Trudeau and Doug Martin unloaded the furniture and supplies in front of the clapboard house on Main Street, residents of the village described their complaints and asked for advice. So, in spite of his reluctance to use his limited strength on practice, Trudeau sent Lottie a long list of medicines to be ordered in New York. He still refused to make out-of-town calls, and did not charge anyone for his services, hoping to keep demands at a minimum. By the time Lottie, the children and nurse Ann Gaffney arrived, nearly everyone in town had discovered a complaint—guides, lumbermen, the barber, and assorted residents who came from nearby settlements.

Apparently it did not occur to any of them that it might be an imposition to ask their new resident to prescribe for animals too. Nor did it seem like one to Trudeau. He had grown so fond of the hunting dogs that he understood when their owners spoke about them as if they were people. One of his early prescriptions called for a mixture of carbolic acid, oil tar, sulphur and olive oil, at the bottom was this notation: *For mange. Rub on dog several times.*

Mr. Edgar was also under Trudeau's care for the winter, and was his only paying charge. It was like old times to use a stethoscope again, and the young physician found that his ear was as keen as ever.

As the winter weather came on, he began to feel really at home in Saranac Lake. The family settled in the simple house which they had rented for twenty-five dollars a month. Again Trudeau's health improved. The woods and surrounding mountains were white now, and even the houses looked less dingy with their roofs decorated by thick blankets of snow. Although Trudeau was eager to make friends in Saranac, he knew that the best way to accomplish this was to allow "old-timers" to make the first advances. Fortunately, his reputation as a dead shot had preceded him, and before long the guides came around to talk with him, to relate stories of hunting. His favorite was a small, wiry guide named Fitz Greene Halleck.

While they were mark shooting behind the Trudeau house one day, Fitz suggested that they form a gun club and offer a prize, a pool of five dollars a member, to the man who killed the biggest rabbit between January 1 and April 1. Trudeau was only too happy to join, and within a few days eight others became charter members of the new club. Milo Miller spread the news, and the contest took on great importance in the quiet community. Meanwhile, Trudeau was interested in acquiring his first rabbit hound.

"I want a dog who will stick to business, not go chasing off on a fox track when I start him after a rabbit," he told Fitz. From his experience at St. Regis, he learned that success in hunting could depend in large measure on the dog.

Fitz finally came in with one, a strange mixture of beagle and foxhound. "Don't look like no beauty, doc, but this little Bunnie is perfect. She'll run the same rabbit all day if she has to."

Even with Bunnie's expert help, the first rabbits the two men brought in for weighing at the store were only three to three and a half pounds. Several weeks later a contestant killed one weighing four pounds.

The chase grew hotter. Fitz was beside himself with anxiety, and Trudeau looked on the match as a matter of great importance to his reputation in Saranac. The chief topic of conversation wherever he went was the weight of the latest rabbit hung outside Miller's store. Each time someone topped the pair's latest kill, Fitz came on the run, insisting that he and Trudeau go out at once.

Lottie also took the contest seriously and looked after Bunnie almost as carefully as she did the two children.

Three days before the deadline, Fitz arrived with the sad news that someone had tipped the beam at four pounds, six ounces—one ounce heavier than Trudeau's latest.

Even Bunnie, who always came out of her snug nest behind the big square kitchen stove when she heard the guide at the back door, sensed the urgency and started to bark. Several days earlier she had gotten her feet in bad shape from running on crusted snow, so Fitz had another dog along. Bunnie insisted on going, and out they went, leaving the new dog behind.

It was snowing hard when they reached the slope at the edge of town, where Fitz said he had seen an "extra-large rabbit" that morning. He drove the sleigh around the hill to a grove of poplars near a small swamp. Trudeau took up his stand while the guide cleared brush and boughs to give a clear view. Bunnie darted into the swamp, her clear, bell-like voice echoing through the leafless trees. Soon she quieted.

Nothing happened for an hour or so while Trudeau waited in the strong wind, shivering with cold. Much as he wanted to go home, the thought of that new rabbit hanging on Miller's store front, with his rival's name attached to one foot, kept him from giving up. He stood there stamping his feet, swinging his arms—hoping.

Suddenly the dog barked, far off to his left.

Fitz, completely out of breath but flushed with happy anticipa-

tion, appeared through the trees. "Come on, get in the sleigh! I want
to move around the hill a ways. Bunnie has that big one on the run!"

Trudeau barely had time to jump out of the sleigh again when he
saw Bunnie, close on the heels of a large rabbit, racing downhill.
He lifted his gun and fired.

The dog stopped howling, sniffed the ground, then ran up to him,
her long tail whipping her rear.

Fitz raised the spring scale high above his head as he came out
of the brush. "Hurry! Not a minute to lose. He's bleeding like
sixty!"

Trudeau untied the reins while Fitz unblanketed the horse.

"Now, run him! This is at least three ounces heavier!"

Trudeau set the mare full speed and raced her toward the village.
He dared not lose a second, for this was probably his last chance to
win the contest. "Out of the way!" he shouted as they turned into
Main Street.

It was unnecessary to tell anyone to move. Every man, woman
and child in sight turned on his heels and made for the store. Dogs
barked, boys screamed, doors flew open. A whole caravan followed
the sleigh. Fitz hopped out and disappeared inside the store before
Trudeau drew in the reins.

Seconds later Fitz reappeared. "Four pounds, eight and one-half
ounces! Lost only an ounce on the way!"

Trudeau hopped out of the sleigh and grabbed the rabbit. "I won!
I won!" No one could top this!

No one did.

A month later, when the Trudeaus left for Paul Smith's, Milo
Miller stopped them on the street. "I just want to say, doc, you're
going to be missed in Saranac. Coming back next fall?"

Trudeau turned to see what his wife would say.

"Of course we are. People are friendly and helpful here. It's been
a wonderful winter for all of us."

Bunnie sat proudly on Trudeau's lap, wagging her tail as he
spoke. "Sure, we will be back. All of us!"

Miller heaved a sigh. "Mighty glad to hear it. It's not just that
we need a real doctor in Saranac. For all your education, you're a

good sport. We take to your kind here in the north woods, doc." He shook hands all around and patted the two children.

"You know," Lottie said as they started up the steep slope toward St. Regis, "I think you won more friends in that contest than you did by all your free medical advice."

Trudeau knew that she was right. In this country the people felt more at home with those who could match them, or would try to match them, in their own skills. It was, as Paul had said, their way of taking your measure. You could not buy their friendship. It had to be earned.

In mid-May the baby Henry, named for his Grandfather Beare, arrived at the hotel in St. Regis, with only Trudeau and Mrs. Smith as attendants. Lottie was fine, the baby was fine, Trudeau was fine. He started the summer in an unusually happy mood, but he made up his mind to rest as much as possible so that Dr. Loomis would see that this regime really helped.

Chatte and Ned were growing rapidly, and their father spent many joyful hours with them. The family lacked only one thing— a church. During the summer at St. Regis various ministers who were in the habit of coming up for vacations took turns holding services in the hotel parlor, but this was not enough for a clergy-man's daughter.

"If we could have a little Episcopal chapel here, and one in Saranac," she told Trudeau soon after Henry's birth, "I would be perfectly contented."

He talked it over with Paul Smith.

"Well, if that's all it takes to make your wife happy in the north woods, let's do something about it. I'll give you a piece of land large enough for the church and cemetery, and the men will bring in good straight logs. The rest is up to you."

This was a generous contribution. With the land and logs as a beginning, Trudeau made plans for raising money to cover the other expenses. His first thought was of Mrs. Livingston and how she loved St. Regis. As he expected, his letter to her brought a generous response. He could count on a thousand dollars, part of it to come from a fair to be held in her New York home. With her name as the first cash donor, he approached various New Yorkers, summer residents who came to him that year for medical advice. Now that he was feeling almost well and looked even better than he felt, a number who would not have called on him as patients the year before showed no hesitation. Luckily, they were able to pay bills—in contrast to the patients at Saranac—but Trudeau asked only small sums, hoping that this would encourage them to make generous donations to the church fund. By August he had all that he needed. One family donated the cost of the plaster, another provided the pews; there were memorial windows, the altar, the linen, the communion service. Lottie chose the name for the square log church—St. John's in the Wilderness.

They dedicated it on September 13, 1877. Trudeau, who was the warden, stood outside to greet the worshipers as they arrived. The parade of boats, newly painted with banners flying, decorated with red, blue, yellow or green pillows, entered the slough and tied up at the new dock. He was excited and happy as he shook hands with the congregation. Every man who entered had in some way contributed to the building of St. John's.

As a medical student, Trudeau had learned the satisfaction of ministering to the destitute; from this experience he learned the joy and satisfaction of asking for donations. Here was the church in the wilderness to show for his small effort—a beautiful, simple log chapel dedicated to God, a watchful superior being who somehow was nearer to reality here on the shore of Lower St. Regis than in the crowded city which these people called home.

The next task would be to build a chapel for Saranac, their winter home, he told himself as he walked to his seat in the front pew.

When he told Lottie this later, she smiled happily. "Of course, you must do that, but somehow I don't think the second church will ever look as beautiful as this, or mean as much to us."

Her words were prophetic, for two months later Baby Henry died, after only two days of illness. He was the first to be placed in the little cemetery beside the chapel. Now, even the ground was to the bereaved parents a hallowed spot. The shadow of St. John's in the Wilderness, and the strong pines outside the windows, sheltered one of their own. Sorrow as well as joy bound them to the north woods. It was now, indeed, their home.

X.

THE DREAM

◘◘◘

During this winter of 1877-78, the Trudeaus lived in a boarding house run by Mrs. Lute Evans, directly across the street from the house they had rented the previous year. It was a fine arrangement, since Mrs. Evans took care of the cooking and housekeeping, leaving Lottie free to spend all of her time with the family. Mrs. Evans was a good-natured woman who made every effort to see that the Trudeaus felt perfectly at home, but she warned them that she did not like dogs. "They may be all right in their place, but not in the house."

Until cold weather set in, Trudeau dutifully kept Bunnie and his new hound Jeff in the woodshed near the kitchen door, but when the night temperatures dropped to near-zero, he brought the dogs inside to snooze in front of the blazing living room fire during the long winter evenings.

Mrs. Evans frowned when she first saw the dogs in forbidden territory, but soon became accustomed to their presence, and during the entire six winters the Trudeaus lived with her, stepped over and around the animals as if they were part of the furniture.

News that Saranac Lake now boasted a resident physician brought a gradual change in the character of the town. A new hotel, accommodating sixteen guests and named the Berkeley, opened its doors for year-round hunters, and Trudeau added a few more patients to his list, although practicing medicine on a full-time basis was still far from his thoughts or hopes.

All of these new patients suffered from phthisis, and since they were well-to-do, accustomed to paying well for medical care, he was able to supplement his and Lottie's small inherited income on a modest scale. Again he decided to keep his charges low, for he was determined to fulfill his promise to beg money for another church. In the spring of this second winter at Saranac he started a subscription campaign for the building of St. Luke, the Beloved Physician. The hotel guests as well as residents of the town donated money, and six months later a lovely Queen Anne-style church with three stained-glass chancel windows representing Faith, Hope and Charity was dedicated. Again Trudeau was named warden.

The family continued to spend their summers at St. Regis, which was still Trudeau's favorite spot in the north woods. His greatest satisfaction came when Dr. Loomis showed him an article to be published in the *Medical Record* during the spring of 1879. In it he quoted Trudeau:

> High mountains, the desert, and the open sea have perhaps given so far the best results in the treatment of chronic chest disease; and yet all these differ widely except in one respect, namely, pure air, which is necessary to diseased lungs.

Loomis made a few comments on his own in this regard, then quoted what was to Trudeau the real point of his own argument: "Pure atmosphere, good food, quiet, *perfect rest* are essential."

As usual in professional articles, Dr. Loomis detailed several case histories. The first was that of Mr. Edgar. This was followed by an account of Trudeau's medical record. It told how he had become ill at the age of twenty-five, of his early attempts to overcome the disease in South Carolina and St. Paul, going on to contrast the results with those of his first two trips to St. Regis. Loomis then spoke of Trudeau's return to the Adirondacks and the condition he was in when Loomis first examined him. Up to this point the account was accurate and objective, but Trudeau was a bit irritated by one statement: "I advised him to remain at St. Regis during the winter, and although he was repeatedly warned such a step would prove fatal, he followed my advice."

His advice? His "consent" was nearer to the truth.

The last section of the article was accurate, and Trudeau was pleased with it, particularly the final paragraph:

> From that time the doctor began slowly to improve. At the present his weight is 158 pounds, a gain of 22 pounds since he first came to the Adirondacks, and 10 pounds more than his weight in health. He presents the appearance of a person in good health. In his lungs evidences still remain of the disease he has so many years combatted. I shall have accomplished my purpose, if by this hastily prepared paper I shall have awakened in my professional brethren the spirit of investigation as regards this extensive health-restoring region.

For the first time Trudeau saw his name in print, in a professional journal, on his special field of study. He wondered whether he should have written the article himself, laying more emphasis on the value of rest, but decided that it was better that Dr. Loomis, so highly respected in medical circles, should pioneer for him. It would make others take notice. The medical profession must change its thinking and adopt new methods in the treatment of phthisis, and the sooner they did so, the better. 149385

Now that Trudeau actually had a "good grip on the tiger," his interest in keeping abreast of the latest developments in medicine grew. He subscribed to several journals and received others through his friend Luis Walton. He watched them carefully for news in his field, now being referred to more generally as "tuberculosis" rather than by the older technical name of phthisis. Nothing really startling appeared until the spring of 1882, in Anstie's *English Practitioner*, which Walton forwarded to him each month. Eddie was astonished to find an account by an English physician of his visit to a sanatorium in Silesia, operated by a German named Dr. Brehmer who suffered from tuberculosis himself.

Brehmer had discovered that a combination of rest, fresh air and minimum exercise was beneficial. The German also believed that the sanatorium was the best place for treatment, since it isolated the patient from family troubles and made recovery from disturbing symptoms easier. He held to the theory that tuberculosis was in some way related to having a small heart.

Trudeau was disgusted when he read this—the old inheritance idea gaining new adherents. Brehmer advocated graded climbing exercises in order to strengthen his patient's heart. It was absolute nonsense!

The English reporter then spoke of a visit to another institution in southern Germany near Frankfort, where a Dr. Dettweiler advocated complete rest and saw no relation between the size of the heart and pulmonary tuberculosis. This was more like it.

During the months that followed Trudeau's discovery of Brehmer and Dettweiler, he kept their theories constantly in mind—even when he was out hunting. He always had plenty of time to think, since he spent many quiet hours on the mountain slopes waiting for Fitz and the dogs to start a fox down one of the runs.

His favorite spot was high on Mount Pisgah, in a pasture where he found a slight depression sheltered from both south and west winds. In this comfortable place he had a beautiful view across the Saranac River toward the forested mountain range, which changed hue constantly in the light and shade of winter afternoons. Sometimes, as he waited, he recalled his youth and mused on the changes his illness had brought, the alternation of setback and improvement. As Dr. Janeway said, this disease had a way of coming back. Trudeau was now thirty-four years old. How many years did he have ahead of him? Sometimes he felt fine and death seemed remote; then he thought of Frank, of how he, too, had his good days. Trudeau knew now that his brother had had no chance for recovery from the day they left Newport. He had been doomed. Then the physician recalled his early clinic patients, the young men and women who were doomed only because of the kind of life they had to lead. "What would this place do for people like that?" he asked.

He imagined that he saw a group of small cottages, especially designed to care for the tuberculous. The Germans had large, hospital-type buildings for their patients, but Trudeau thought his idea was better, less institutional. It would be more homelike and pleasant —and easier to secure funds for, of course. He could build one at a time, as the need arose and the money came. He visualized people bundled in robes and fur caps, sheltered from the cold winds, sitting as he was now, gradually winning their battles against the stubborn disease—no worries, good food, good clean air and *rest*. And as the winter passed, the dream continued to develop until at last he spoke of it to Lottie.

"I'm surprised that you kept it to yourself so long. That's not like you, Eddie."

"Well, I guess it seemed so unreal at first." That was the only reason he could think of offhand.

"A fine idea. Would it cost a lot of money?"

That was the problem. But as Trudeau thought about the poor people in New York, the sufferers who could not afford the luxury of a hotel or even a boardinghouse, he knew that there must be some solution, for a few of them at least. He wanted to help young men and women who must surely die if they stayed in their crowded, smoky, noisy tenements. He had raised money before. To make his dream come true he would do it again . . . He would save the lives of people who had tuberculosis in the early stages, when they were most likely to respond to sanatorium treatment.

Until now there had been few men with whom he could talk about medicine during the long winters in Saranac Lake, but in 1882 D. W. Riddle arrived, a good businessman with experience in building and a reader of medical literature. He showed a lively interest in Trudeau's plan for a sanatorium and offered to take charge of construction when and if money became available. Also, there was Charles M. Lea, the medical-book publisher from Philadelphia, who brought his ailing wife to Saranac Lake. He, too, liked the idea.

But this was getting ahead of the schedule. Trudeau's first move should be a talk with Dr. Loomis; it was essential to gain his support.

When the New York physician arrived to spend the summer in his new cottage, which Paul Smith had built for him only a short walk from the hotel, Trudeau spoke of his dream, beginning cautiously in order to avoid the danger of an outright veto. "You and I agree that this country is ideal for consumptives, but it seems too bad that poor sick people cannot take advantage of it. Do you agree?"

Loomis frowned. "Of course, of course. But that is always the case with the poor. They must be content with what the clinics provide."

Trudeau wished to avoid an argument, but he felt that the best strategy was to speak his mind at once. "I've been reading about the Germans and their sanatorium methods. It's small wonder that nearly all the consumptive patients at Bellevue die young. Now, if I could get enough money, even to build just one or two cottages and care for cases which are not too advanced, charge only a small fee for maintenance—well—I think it would be a good test of the sanatorium theory. What do you say, doctor?"

Loomis had evidently found time to get over his surprise. "Yes, I believe it might well prove an interesting experiment, instructive to specialists in our field. As you know, this is of vital interest to me. My only question is, how do you finance this experiment?"

"Through begging. I want nothing for myself, merely an opportunity to prove the theory to other physicians."

"Where do I come in?" Loomis asked.

This was going to take nerve, but it was best to speak boldly. "I hope you will consent to be our representative. Would you be willing to screen patients in New York when we are ready?"

"Of course, of course." Dr. Loomis smiled. "I would be happy to do that little job. I fear we will meet some opposition. And money never comes easily for any charity. I wish you good luck in your begging. You can count on my support from the medical angle. It could prove a most helpful experiment to the profession."

Trudeau was so happy that he shook hands and left immediately to tell the good news to Lottie.

That evening they set up a plan for the fund-raising campaign.

"I suggest that you begin just as you did when you asked money for St. John's, Eddie. Speak first to someone up here who has influence. Once you have a prominent name in your subscription book, the others will be more willing to give."

"You mean that I should ask Paul Smith first?"

"Oh no," his wife said. "Nor do I think you should begin with your friend Mrs. Louis Livingston. This is more complicated, too much so, too important to trust to a mere letter. Look around among the summer residents. Find someone who is the sympathetic type and has money as well as influence."

Trudeau slept fitfully that night—which he always did when he had something on his mind—but by morning he had made his decision. He would approach Anson Phelps Stokes, a man with a large family, greatly admired. Two of his children had been in poor health, with signs of early tuberculosis. Two summers in the Adirondacks had done wonders for them. He was sure to listen and, best of all, Eddie was going fishing with him today on Spitfire Lake. He would wait until they were ready to come back that afternoon.

He began warily, for if he could convince Mr. Stokes, it would mean that he had a talking point with others whom this man knew well. Trudeau spoke of the wonderful bracing air. Did Mr. Stokes agree that it made even a healthy person feel better?

"Yes indeed!"

"You must look forward to coming here to your camp each summer. It's too bad so few can do this, isn't it, Mr. Stokes?"

"Yes."

Mr. Stokes' handsome, mustached face was almost expressionless, but Trudeau decided to press his point. "There must be thousands of people in New York who desperately need such a place as this."

"Yes."

At least the reaction was pleasant, so Trudeau plunged into his story. He went on to tell about his agreement with Dr. Loomis, his plan to take no salary for himself and to charge only a few dollars a week for maintenance. Any deficit would have to be made up through donations. They reached the shore at this point in the discourse. Trudeau wanted to say more, but he thought he had gone far enough for a first attempt. He must give the man a chance to think it over.

Mr. Stokes tied up the *Delos*. They stood at the shoreline, looking across the broad expanse of water. In the far distance a flock of wild geese soared high. Several white clouds rode in the breeze. The lake was a deep blue, reflecting the sky. Mr. Stokes stood motionless, a faraway look in his fine eyes. Suddenly he turned.

"If you decide to carry out your plan, doctor, call on me for five hundred dollars."

Trudeau was so surprised that he shook his companion's hand

until his own arm ached. "Oh thanks, thanks!" He reached in his vest pocket and pulled out a small notebook. At the top of the first page he wrote *Mr. Anson Phelps Stokes—$500.00.*

A few minutes later he jumped in his own boat and rowed back to his camp, happier than he had been in months. Next winter, when he and Fitz rode up to their favorite fox run, it would be like going home. Who owned that old pasture anyway?

Gradually the fund built up during the summer—five dollars, ten dollars, two hundred dollars.

Trudeau shuddered at the thought of approaching perfect strangers for donations, but Mr. Stokes had warned him that if he expected to succeed in establishing even a small institution he would need to call on many rich men. He had given him the name of a D. Willis James in New York as a starter.

In November the Trudeaus journeyed to the city. It was a strange sensation, returning to this scene of so much happiness, hope and despair, but hope was the strongest of Trudeau's emotions as he stood on the steps of 40 East 39th Street, the brownstone house where Mr. James lived. Would the rich New Yorker treat him like a troublesome book agent?

Ushering Trudeau into a handsome parlor, the butler said he would announce him. Trudeau sat on the edge of the rosewood sofa, nervously fingering his black broadcloth coat.

In a moment a kindly faced middle-aged gentleman wearing a swallow-tailed coat entered with outstretched hand. "Dr. Trudeau? Oh yes, a friend of Mr. Stokes. He mentioned your name the other day. What can I do for you?"

Trudeau jumped up and began to talk, giving some of his own background. Then he said, "I have come to ask for money, sir. I want to build a little hospital for consumptives in the Adirondacks."

Mr. James smiled. "Sit down, doctor. Now, begin at the beginning and tell me all about your plans."

Trudeau began again, but his voice sounded far away, as if it belonged to someone else. He was not sure that what he said made sense, but he talked on and on. When he paused for a second, he saw that Mr. James wanted to say something.

"May I have a look at the names of those who have signed?"

Trudeau fumbled in his coat pocket and handed over the book, half expecting the man to laugh at the small amounts that most of the people had given.

Without changing expression, Mr. James went to his desk, pulled out his checkbook, dipped his pen and wrote: *Twenty-five hundred dollars.* Then he said, "I am deeply grateful to you for this great privilege, a most worthy cause. The best of luck to you, doctor."

On the way to the Belmont Hotel, Trudeau marveled at his success. How pleasant that interview had been. Aglow, he stopped to see several physicians who had lucrative practices in New York, men in a position to give money or at least suggest names of those who might find the cause appealing. But to his chagrin, the reactions were all negative.

"I do not know what you are driving at," one of the doctors said. "Consumption is incurable. Why ask money for an idea like that? There are plenty of charity beds in our hospitals."

"Sounds most depressing," another said. "An aggregation of hopeless invalids forty-two miles from a railroad. Awful!"

"This is altogether visionary, Trudeau," said a third. "The climate is too damp and cold. Well, here is five dollars."

The last of the group said, "A doctor in Asheville, North Carolina, had a hare-brained idea similar to this. Those Germans have done a lot of harm with that plan of theirs. Asheville failed. So will you."

Trudeau was downcast, but he would not give up. When he and Lottie returned to Saranac Lake two weeks later, he had five thousand dollars to add to the fund—enough to start building the caretaker's house, which would include bedrooms for patients and sanatorium office as well as a small barn nearby. The cottages would come later. Of this he was positive. Nothing would stop him now, absolutely nothing.

The rough, boulder-strewn, sloping pasture and fox run belonged to a Preacher Smith, he learned from Fitz Greene Halleck. The guide had, at Trudeau's request, done some quiet sleuthing and believed that Smith might sell about sixteen acres of it. "But must you buy *this* land?" he asked. "I could easily find another place just as good for your hospital."

Charles Lea, who was visiting his ill wife, agreed with Fitz. He suggested that a spot nearer to town might be better, more accessible.

Trudeau was insistent. "This pasture is the only place I have seen around here that has a fine view as well as protection from strong winds. I know! Fitz and I have hunted on every slope in the neighborhood. Preacher Smith's pasture is only a mile and a half from town. No, I want to build there."

Mr. Lea and Fitz made no further suggestion.

A few days later the guide returned. He and the other guides, including several whom Trudeau scarcely knew, had chipped in and paid four hundred dollars for the Mount Pisgah pasture.

"This is the devil of a way to spoil our best fox run!" Fitz said as he handed over the check.

XI.

A STARTLING ANNOUNCEMENT

Eager though Trudeau was to get the sanatorium started, he had to wait until plans could be drawn, materials and workmen arranged for and a farmer persuaded to do the maintenance work and provide board for patients. All this was in Mr. Riddle's capable hands. Meanwhile, another major project loomed on the horizon.

Chatte was now ten years old, a blonde, plump, athletic girl with many friends and interests. Ned, a year younger but tall and slender, was also active, and these two often brought confusion to the Evans boardinghouse.

Not that Mrs. Evans objected, but Lottie felt that the time had come for them to have a house of their own, where there would be room for guests as well as privacy for Trudeau's small medical practice. His cousin and companion of Rockwood days, Larry Aspinwall, now known as J. Lawrence Aspinwall, was an architect in New York City. He and his sister Minnie visited the Trudeaus at St. Regis during the summers and showed an interest in all the family's hopes. Minnie was as volatile as ever, and her brother, who was pudgy and serious, offered to help. Trudeau was grateful for their support.

Aspinwall's first task had been to direct the building of an addition to St. John's in the Wilderness. He now drew up plans for the Trudeaus' house in Saranac Lake. Like St. Luke's, across the street at the corner of Church and Main streets, the home was Queen Anne in style, two-storied, with a room twelve by eight feet which had two small closets at the back of the house to serve as an office. The stable was to be at one side of the lot.

Trudeau spent many happy hours in his small office seeing patients and reading ever more widely in his field of medicine. He still went hunting and fishing, but less often than during his first six years at Saranac and had almost no time to spend with the children now. His practice and plans absorbed his energy. His hours with Fitz served more as a restorative when he was tired or nervous or worried over a patient who did not respond to his rest treatment.

His many years of isolation in the wilderness trying to restore his own health had caused him to fall behind in his field of medicine, and he sorely missed contacts with other physicians.

This was the beginning of the new era in experimental medicine. The great French chemist Louis Pasteur had proven that there was no such thing as spontaneous development of bacteria. Even before Trudeau had entered college Joseph Lister showed that antiseptics could prevent wound infections. The Parisian, J. A. Villemin, had been able to innoculate with tuberculous tissue to produce the disease in both men and animals, but his theory that phthisis, or tuberculosis, was caused by a germ was still unverified. Dr. Austin Flint was one of the few American physicians who had long maintained that the disease was due to a germ. But until this could be proven, everyone must work in the dark. How could you find a cure when you did not know the cause? That was the great problem, and

Trudeau knew that until that day came, his work with tuberculous patients lacked a firm, scientific foundation.

He was thumbing through a copy of the English periodical, *The Practitioner*, for May, 1882, when he came across a startling announcement in the back of the magazine, on page 375. It contained in an extract from another journal, a summary of a report by Dr. Robert Koch, who, as an obscure German physician, had worked in a small laboratory at the back of his office during his early years. Koch had been a student of Jacob Henle, a German scientist who in 1840 had decided that most infections were caused by minute parasitical organisms, and had set up methods for proving his contention. Using his master's postulates, Koch had finally proved that, in the case of anthrax in cattle, the disease was caused by a specific bacteria. This discovery made Koch famous and he was able to move to Berlin, where he established his large laboratory and surrounded himself with assistants, mostly students and young physicians. It was here that he worked on the problem of phthisis.

The announcement stated that, "Koch has apparently succeeded at last not only in recognizing the tubercle virus, but in cultivating it artificially."

The magazine fell out of Trudeau's hands onto the desk. He sat for a moment staring straight ahead of him, then snatched the periodical again and with shaking fingers reopened it to page 375.

Yes, that was right. *It said that this German named Koch had identified the cause of tuberculosis.* He had cultivated this bacillus outside the body! But how? Eagerly, Trudeau read on.

Koch used methylene blue and vesuvin to stain his specimens. These words meant nothing to Trudeau. He hurried along down the page.

> The tubercle bacteria remains blue after staining, it is rodlike in shape and belongs to the group of bacilli, very thin, about the diameter of a red blood corpuscle as seen under the microscope. It generally forms in bundles but free bacilli appear at the edges of the tissues as the disease spreads.

This bacillus alone causes the disease, Koch stated.

Trudeau recalled that in reading about the inventor of the stethoscope, Laënnec, he had learned that this scientist believed that all forms of tuberculosis had a common cause. Now Koch had proven the unitary theory to be correct. All forms of the disease in humans came from this one bacillus!

Koch insisted that the cavities and tubercles could not grow where no bacillus was present. He believed that dust and sputum carried the germ, and that it probably entered the body through inhalation! Good old Dr. Flint was right after all.

Trudeau did not know even the first principles of the new science of bacteriology. He had never stained a specimen in his life, for in school this was considered outside the province of medical students. Somehow he must duplicate the Koch experiments, verify this claim himself. Too excited to think clearly, he talked to Lottie about his problem. She suggested that the next time they went to New York to solicit funds he find someone to teach him how to perform the necessary experiments.

Meanwhile, he would try to get hold of the Koch article. He was positive that it contained the full details. The German had found the cause of phthisis—he had seen it under the microscope. He knew how to grow it. He could bring on the disease in other animals. Hopefully Trudeau searched every periodical on his desk. There were two brief statements. That was all.

He realized more than ever what a handicap his isolation was. It was a temptation to go to New York at once, but he restrained himself. He must first write to Luis Walton and try to find out what the men in the city were saying about all this. When Dr. Loomis arrived at St. Regis in a few weeks he would ask him too.

Luis replied that, except for Dr. Flint, no one was very excited. Janeway wanted to read the entire report before committing himself. Dr. Loomis' comment was, "I cannot add anything. The complete report has not been published in this country. To be truthful, I do not much believe in germs."

Not believe in germs? Eddie was tempted to argue, but immediately recalled something Grandfather Berger once said: "The scientific mind is always cautious. This is the history of medical progress. The general public is always ahead of the physicians in accepting new medical theories. They are ahead because they do not know enough to be cautious."

If Dr. Loomis went so far as to reject the germ theory, naturally he would show little interest in the Koch announcement. Trudeau knew that he had taken a big step ahead of most medical men in accepting the rest and fresh-air treatment for tuberculosis. No doubt Loomis' conservatism had contributed to his reputation as a sound medical practitioner. He was too busy, too wrapped up in his practice to spend time in a laboratory, blindly trying to duplicate the Koch experiments. There were many like him.

As for Edward Livingston Trudeau, he wanted to practice *and* experiment, for he now saw the problem of tuberculosis as bound up in both disciplines.

His friend Charles Lea made a sensible suggestion: "Let's get hold of the Koch paper. You would be wasting time and energy if you went to New York before reading the entire report. You must first know how Koch got his results, see whether they appear valid."

"Can you get a copy of the report?"

"Yes, it may have reached our Philadelphia office by now. It will be in German, of course." There was a look of amusement on Lea's small round face.

Trudeau wilted. "I don't read German."

"Never mind, I'll get it translated."

For the first time Trudeau wished that he had taken German seriously at the Lycée. He had wriggled out of it after only one year because the language had irritated him. How could he have known that he would ever need to know German?

True to his promise, the publisher had the paper translated and presented it to Trudeau as a Christmas gift—three hundred pages in longhand.

First, Koch pointed out the failures of past students in trying to solve the riddle of tuberculosis. He sketched the long history, the generally accepted theory that the disease resulted from constitutional peculiarities rather than from direct contagion. Koch's problem "was to determine whether some microorganism was the cause, to see whether, if this were so, it had independent life."

The scientist described the methods he used in his Berlin experiments, and these Trudeau read slowly and carefully. Next came the steps used in innoculating animals and producing the disease in their bodies. Sections of the paper dealt with various kinds of tuberculosis—of the lungs, bone, glands and other organs.

It was wonderful! A magnificent report, so clear, so logical and exhaustive. Every word fascinated Trudeau, although much of the description bearing on experiments continued to puzzle him, for he scarcely knew which end of a test tube was which. As he recalled this sad fact, he fell into a depressed mood.

Of course he had his grandfather's microscope out on the desk in his office. This was his one and only piece of equipment. He had no books to help teach him how to do experiments. Nothing. How was he to begin? After careful thought he decided that his first task was to learn how to prepare specimens, how to stain them and recognize the tubercle bacillus under his microscope. Only then could he test Koch's conclusions, using sputum obtained from his patients. It was difficult to restrain his imagination, to keep from soaring off into the future, to dream of finding a cure for mankind's greatest killer.

"If I can just verify Koch's theory, I will have done something," he told Lottie, trying to calm himself.

His wife looked worried.

"What's the matter? Don't you think I'm smart enough?"

"You know better than to ask that. My worry is, dear, are you strong enough?"

"Of course I am. Most people never know I've been sick until someone tells them. I look the picture of health."

Lottie gave him a sidelong glance. "Your looks are deceiving. If you're so healthy, why is it you tire easily? And are nervous? I heard you prowling around the house last night. You never sleep an entire night through. Lately you've been complaining of headaches. Sometimes you are edgy with the children."

Trudeau started to protest, but she interrupted.

"Now, of course, when a bunch of them get to talking and dancing around in the parlor, they irritate *me*. But when you're overtired you're invariably cross. They understand. Don't worry about it, Eddie." She rose from her chair and came over to his, kissed him, smiled and left the room.

He sat down in the chair by the front window to think. Lottie was always fair, even though at times she was overanxious. He was undertaking a great deal for a man with his history of poor health. Although he seldom complained, at times he was worried about himself. Extra exertion tired him. There were the plans for the sanatorium—the main building was almost finished. He now had money to build the first cottage, which would be a small frame building with a porch on the front. Mr. Riddle warned that he must step up his efforts since the institution would cost more and more to operate as it developed. There were his winter patients in town and the summer guests at St. Regis to be taken care of, and now his plans for setting up a laboratory and learning from scratch all he must know to perform the experiments. It gave him a headache to think of all that lay ahead. But he could hardly wait to get started.

November, 1883, the date set for his next "begging" trip to New York, finally arrived. As soon as Lottie was settled in Douglaston he went into the city to see Luis Walton. His friend was deeply interested in his plan, for he, too, had now read the entire Koch report, but since he was practicing among others at least as well informed as he was, he knew the tenor of their thinking.

"Most of the men are cagey or downright hostile. I do not agree with them, but I think you should know what you are up against."

Trudeau could hardly believe that the great physicians of New York could be so slow to see the implications of the Koch experiments, to accept the possibility that he was right and be willing to change their way of thinking. Loomis was not an exception. As Trudeau hurried from one office to the next, at first with buoyant hopes, then gradually with a weary recognition of the hard road ahead of him, he heard over and over as he spoke of his plans:

"Go slow, you are too young and enthusiastic."

"You must not risk your professional standing."

"How can you verify Koch way off in a wilderness with no help?"

"Leave test tubes to the bacteriologists and chemists. A doctor has no time for such things. Who is that little German Koch to say we are wrong?"

Finally, after Trudeau had made the rounds with encouragement from only two men—Janeway and Flint—he went back to see Luis.

"Go over to the town office of Dr. George Peabody. You know him. He brought in a new man to teach pathology at the college. The name is Dr. T. Mitchell Prudden, and he worked with Koch in Berlin for a while."

Trudeau knew Peabody well, for he was related by marriage to the Livingstons. It took only a minute to get a card of introduction to the professor of pathology, then he hurried to the College of Physicians and Surgeons.

The college was still the same. Even the secretary was there—solemn, curt, still treating him as if he were a student.

"Dr. Prudden is in his laboratory," he said without looking up from the stack of papers he was shuffling.

"Where is the laboratory?"

"Outside on the street level."

The room next to the ice-cream parlor looked vacant at first. The windows were grimy, and a dark green curtain covered the glass door panel. Two small boys squatted in front of the iron grating.

"Oh, golly, look! What's that he's got in the sink?" one of them asked, a mixture of horror and glee in his piping voice.

"A heart!" replied the other, shivering. "No, I guess it's a liver. Looks like a liver. Do you suppose it came out of a man or a woman?"

"Neither, silly. Probably out of a monkey."

Trudeau opened the door and stepped inside. The stench of alcohol, pickled flesh and cigar smoke in the closed, narrow, high-ceilinged room almost knocked him down. He looked around: in front of him was a potbellied stove with a kettle of water sizzling on its small top, and beyond that a long, low table where several students sat in front of microscopes, talking in low tones. The walls of the room were lined with shelves, evidently left over from an earlier proprietor. On them were variously colored bottles—large, small, square, squat, tall and fat, all bearing small labels. At the front was a sink where a tall, fine-looking young man smoking a huge cigar wielded a scalpel.

He looked up. "Oh, I thought it was a student. We seldom have visitors." He quickly washed his hands and dried them on his black apron as he came forward. "I'm Dr. Eugene Hodenpyl, Dr. Prudden's assistant."

"My name is Trudeau. I have a card from Dr. Peabody. I practice medicine in Saranac Lake."

Dr. Hodenpyl was obviously confused by this information, although he smiled pleasantly.

"I need some advice. Where could I find Dr. Prudden?"

"One minute." The young doctor walked to the far end of the room, climbed a few steep steps and disappeared through a hole into a boxlike compartment which hung from the ceiling. In a moment he reappeared. "He says to come up."

Trudeau hastily mounted the steps. He found a slightly built, sensitive-looking man seated at a table by a window. The room was a maze of test tubes, beakers, slides, boxes, small stoves, incubators and microscopes. He looked for a chair, but there was only one.

Dr. Prudden did not rise, and he looked as if he resented this intrusion. "What can I do for you?"

He nodded when Trudeau spoke of Koch, and listened carefully enough as he heard the request.

"We have microscopes for the use of students down there. You are free to use one as long as it is not needed. Dr. Hodenpyl will explain the method of making sections and staining. Good day, Dr. Trudeau."

If he had not been so determined to see this thing through, Trudeau might have been tempted to give up after this curt interview, but he immediately went down to the laboratory and took a seat at the long table in front of a microscope.

Dr. Hodenpyl brought a small specimen. "This contains the tubercle bacillus. It has already been hardened. Now, come with me and I will show you where the stains are."

He rattled on, explaining how to stain the tissue.

Trudeau was lost almost immediately. "I never did this kind of thing when I was a student here."

Dr. Hodenpyl stared at him. "Oh, I see, of course." He brought out pencil and paper and began to write out the directions.

Trudeau had little trouble learning to harden the specimens, but cutting with the instrument that Hodenpyl called a microtome was difficult at first. The next step was to mount the sections and after that to stain them. He found that he used either too much or too little stain, and a large amount of the deep purplish-blue landed on him. His shoes, his hands, even his face and hair were spotted.

Fortunately Dr. Hodenpyl was understanding and amused him with stories about his own early failures and awkwardness. Still, it was embarrassing to watch the students do so easily what to Trudeau was a nerve-wracking task. He worked from morning until nightfall. Frequently his head ached, and he broke out in a cold sweat before the day was over.

Dr. Prudden finally paused during one of his whirlwind trips between the door and his bird nest. "I see you're still here."

"Well, yes, but I'm not very bright. You see, I never took a course in this kind of thing. Perhaps I was too optimistic . . ."

"Well, at least you're persistent. That goes a long way in this work." Dr. Prudden sat down at the table and peered through the glass. "Too much stain."

After nearly two weeks of work, with no time off for fund-raising, Trudeau finally felt that he knew something. He succeeded in preparing a specimen from the beginning. At last the rodlike chains of bacilli were distinct—a rosy color with a contrasting blue field surrounding them. He was so excited that Dr. Hodenpyl and two of the students came over to congratulate him.

"Now, what must I buy to send back to Saranac? All I have is a microscope, and it's old."

Dr. Hodenpyl made a long list—crystals, hematoxylin from Merck's; gun cotton from Meyrowitz, also a microtome. He must purchase a supply of glass test tubes, beakers and slides.

Trudeau trotted around from one supply house to the other, and after one day had everything ready to ship. He again went to the college to thank Dr. Prudden and Dr. Hodenpyl for their assistance.

Even the students gathered around to shake his hand.

"If you need any information, just write to us," Dr. Prudden said. "It's a pleasure to find a practicing physician who shows an interest in our work. Come back when you're in New York. We—that is, Eugene—will help you. He knows as much about this as I do."

Trudeau hurried to the station to meet Lottie, a broad smile on his face. He could hardly wait to tell her about his success, about his purchases, about his plans for his own small laboratory.

"You must have talked someone out of five thousand dollars," she said as he ran to her and took her bag.

Money? He had completely forgotten about it. "Better than that! I undertook a year's course in bacteriology and passed it in just two weeks! Oh Lottie, it's hard to believe. That tubercle bacillus is so small, so harmless-looking, so difficult to isolate. Just keeping it alive in the test tube is a job. Yet, it is so hard to kill inside the body . . . Strange."

When they were seated in the coach, he asked, "Do you suppose that I will find a way to kill it without harming my patients?"

"I know that you'll try." She gently patted his hand.

He leaned back to rest his head. He closed his eyes, but not to sleep. Every turn of the train wheels sounded the challenge—to try, to try, to try!

XII.

A LAMP IN THE WILDERNESS

Trudeau was tired after the forty-mile drive from the railroad terminus to Saranac Lake, but he had no desire to rest. He dragged Lottie and the children into his twelve-by-eight office to show them just how he expected to turn it into a laboratory. "I can put my apparatus in these two closets, and the microscope will stay on the table, of course. Then I will get someone to rig up a thermostat. That can go in one of the closets too."

"What will you do with your patients?" Lottie asked.

Chatte giggled. "I guess he'll examine them in the kitchen."

"What's a thermostat?" Ned asked.

Trudeau was delighted to see that his son showed an interest in his project. "Sit down and I will draw a picture of one."

The next morning Trudeau appeared at the tinsmith's shop in the local hardware store before it opened for the day. He had to stand in the cold for fifteen minutes, waiting for the proprietor. If only he could afford a thermostat like the new one at Dr. Prudden's laboratory! It had a self-regulating apparatus, with a thermometer that turned the gas heat on and off as needed. But even if he could afford it now, it would be useless, since Saranac Lake had neither gas nor coal. He must grow bacteria with the help of a kerosene lamp for heating the thermostat.

"Now, I want you to send for some sheets of copper," he explained to the sleepy tinsmith. "Make one small box. Cut a tube large enough to hold a large thermometer. I will fill the space around it with water."

To allow easy reading of the temperature, the thermometer itself would poke outside the top of the box, through a pierced cork. He had rummaged around Chatte's room and found her old toy kerosene lamp. It was ideal—small enough to fit under the apparatus.

Although in theory this sounded simple, complications arose, especially at night when the room temperature dropped and the lamp could not keep the water hot enough to prevent the delicate bacilli from dying.

Ned, who was greatly interested in his father's experiments, suggested that they take turns stoking the fire at night, but his mother was against this idea.

"You should be able to find some other way to handle this problem."

Trudeau promptly ordered three wooden boxes, graded in size, with sawdust packed between the spaces as insulation. There were doors in all three of them. "If I open or shut these doors one at a time, depending on the weather, the thermostat will operate at a fairly uniform heat."

Lottie had a wry smile on her face. "Except when there's a very great drop in temperature during the night. That potbellied stove will still have to be stoked when that happens."

A few days later she hired a man to stoke the fire. Trudeau decided that if pure living cultures of the bacillus were the result, it would be worth the added expense. So far, all of them had died, in spite of his repeated efforts and loss of sleep.

Before he could cultivate pure cultures, he must first verify the Koch claim that this bacillus alone caused phthisis. At the moment he had thirty patients whose chest examinations showed positively that they suffered from the disease. All of them were at least moderately advanced cases, with afternoon fevers, coughs, perpetual tiredness, difficulty in maintaining normal weight—the obvious array of symptoms. In twenty-one of the individual samples taken from these patients, he found tubercle bacilli on the first attempt. Eight others had to be tested over a period of two weeks before he found them. One case—a middle-aged woman with clearly advanced phthisis—showed negative sputum for two months, even though he tested daily.

Dr. Prudden had pointed out the necessity for protecting his specimens from outside contamination, so Trudeau collected the sputum in sterilized bottles he capped with sterilized cotton plugs.

While he was engrossed in these beginning experiments, Fitz and the dogs cooled their heels, hoping that the doctor would give up this queer business and take time for a hunting trip. But Trudeau ignored their pleas, putting them off with a promise to go out with them as soon as he had finished these first experiments.

The guide was sitting by the kitchen stove one morning when Trudeau came into the room with a faraway look in his eyes. "Fitz, can you get me a dozen full-grown rabbits right away?"

Bunnie and Jeff raced to the cupboard where their chains hung. Fitz looked up. "You mean you're hungering for rabbit stew?"

"No, certainly not."

"Going to have a party?"

Trudeau laughed. "Oh, I should have explained, I want *live* rabbits. I need them for my laboratory. Can you trap them?"

Fitz sighed. "Oh sure, but I said to your missus only yesterday, you haven't been hunting in weeks. And she said . . ."

"Never mind what Mrs. Trudeau said, Fitz. I must have twelve healthy rabbits, right away. How about it?"

Several days later Fitz drove the cutter up to the back door and unloaded a large crate containing the rabbits.

Meanwhile, Trudeau and Ned had finished building their hutches. As soon as the rabbits had become accustomed to the new surroundings, Trudeau set to work sterilizing his hypodermic needles. He put the animals to sleep with ether, then punctured the back of each right eye and neck of four rabbits, inoculating them with sputum containing the tubercle bacilli. Four others received sputum from patients who had only acute bronchitis. The remaining four were inoculated with samples from the patient who had advanced tuberculosis but no bacilli in her sputum.

From this point on he watched the rabbits with increasing attention, examining them every day for signs of tuberculosis. At the end of eight weeks the first four rabbits died. A post-mortem examination showed that the bacilli affected not only the eyes and shoulders of each rabbit but other organs as well. The animals that received inoculations from the bacillus-free tuberculous patient's sputum remained healthy. So did those animals injected with sputum from the bronchitis patients. To Trudeau this was conclusive, but just to make sure of his findings, he repeated the experiments with guinea pigs—with the same results.

The guinea pigs proved difficult to keep alive, with or without inoculations, for they could not stand cold weather. In order to keep them from dying, he dug a large hole in the yard, equipped it with wooden shelves and heated it with a large kerosene lamp. It was an awkward place to get into, but worth the trouble. At last he verified, without question, the Koch findings. Only the tubercle bacillus could induce tuberculosis.

Trudeau's report summarizing his lengthy experiments was published in *The American Journal of the Medical Sciences* early in 1885, the first research article published in this country supporting the German's startling claim. It marked the beginning of the long series of laboratory experiments that would make an outstanding contribution to the knowledge of tuberculosis. His laboratory would be the first in the United States devoted exclusively to the study of tuberculosis.

The article was only four pages long: "All evidence points to the necessity for the presence of the bacillus in order to produce this disease artificially," it began. If any one should doubt that the woman whose sputum did not contain it really had tuberculosis, Trudeau said that he would stake his reputation on the claim that she had. He pointed out that since the experiments were completed, she had grown worse. He believed hers to be a rare case in a patient with advanced tuberculosis. She could not pass the infection on to others through her sputum.

Trudeau was now so enthusiastic over his ability to detect the bacillus that he established a routine of sputum examination with everyone who had even a slight cough. He was now even more conscious of the danger of contagion, and insisted that his patients cover their mouths during coughing spells. There must be a free flow of clean, fresh air in the sickroom. Some people complained that he was overcautious, and a few were disgusted when he directed them to spit into one of his sterilized jars.

During the following summer at St. Regis a young Harvard College student came to him complaining of a cough and loss of weight. "Dr. Loomis is away on a hunting trip, and he told me before he left to see you if my cough did not let up. Here I am."

Trudeau looked at the tall, athletic figure. Except for a slightly drawn look around the eyes, he certainly looked healthy. "How long have you had this cough? Did it begin with a heavy cold?"

"Yes, I had a cold last March." The student dropped into a chair. "It lasted a month, then gradually cleared up—but the cough stayed. Just hangs on. I thought you might give me some medicine. Father says I can't go hunting until I get rid of it."

"Your father is wise. Now, let me listen to your chest." Trudeau pulled out his stethoscope and went over the young man, back and front. "I cannot hear any *râles*—still, it's strange that your cough persists. You are not subject to asthma? Well, take this small bottle and spit into it when you get up in the morning. Clear your throat. Bring the specimen to me."

The student appeared puzzled. "What about the cough medicine?"

"I'll give that to you tomorrow." Actually, Trudeau did not expect to find any bacillus. The young man was no doubt tired from his hard year at school. He could have a touch of bronchitis. However, he did find several telltale loose rods on his slide the next day. The diagnosis was certain. Strange as it had been to find no *râles*, he knew that the student had tuberculosis.

When the boy was seated in his office the following day, Trudeau asked him a few more questions, then said, "You would be most unwise to return to Harvard this fall. Could you take a year off?"

"A whole year? Why, that is silly . . ."

The time had come to speak plainly. "I advise this because it would be dangerous to your future and to that of your fellow students. Your sputum carries the tubercle bacillus. I suggest that you go to a sunny, dry climate like Colorado where you can live quietly, rest a lot and stay out of doors."

Loomis had told him that some doctors were advising their patients to go to the mountain states since the sunny winter days permitted almost continuous outdoor living. Trudeau would have liked to take on this case here in the Adirondacks, but for ethical reasons could not make the suggestion. The young man was not seriously ill. No doubt the change of climate and routine, the freedom from strain and healthy living would restore him.

It was always difficult to tell anyone that he had tuberculosis, but to a man who thought he had a stubborn cold, this was bound to be a shock. "I, I . . . well, would you talk to my father?"

Trudeau had planned to make several calls in the neighborhood before noon, but he promised to wait until his patient returned with his father.

"Look at him!" the older man said. "Big and strong. He cannot have tuberculosis. All he needs is cough medicine."

Trudeau had heard all this before. If these had been his own patients he would have put it to them bluntly. "Suppose we wait until Dr. Loomis returns."

"We'll do just that! I *trust* his opinion," the father said.

When Trudeau told Dr. Loomis of his findings, the New York physician went at once to the hotel to see the young man. He reported that he heard no *râles*. "You mean to say that you base all this on those bacilli?"

"That is correct."

"Oh come, Trudeau. This is no proof. No, I think you're wrong."

Loomis was obviously disgusted. He said his patient would return to college as he planned.

Unfortunately there was nothing more to say, at least to Dr. Loomis, but Trudeau sputtered about it for several days to Lottie. Four months later one of his patients at Saranac Lake told him that the boy had suffered a serious hemorrhage while attending class and was now on his way to Colorado. There was no joy in saying, "I told you so."

Trudeau did expect a letter from Dr. Loomis containing this news, but none came. How strange it was that really fine students of the disease, men like Loomis who had a national reputation and were expert at detecting tuberculosis with their stethoscopes, should ignore the importance of these tests. Many physicians admitted that germs caused other diseases. Why couldn't they see that it was also true with this one? Apparently his carefully worded article had convinced none of the great physicians in New York—the men he most wanted to convince.

The horizon was not wholly dark, however. Several north-woods physicians showed an interest in his article. Trudeau received a letter from a Dr. D'Avignon at Ausable Forks. He knew the physician-surgeon slightly and believed that he was unusually shrewd and skillful. It was nice to learn that Dr. D'Avignon would visit him during the coming winter.

Meanwhile, the combination office-laboratory had begun to resemble Dr. Prudden's bird nest. Not that Trudeau minded, but after several patients stained their clothes and objected to the "awful smell," he had to do something drastic. He had workmen build a small room adjacent to the old one. It was almost the same size, but afforded him a chance to arrange his equipment to better advantage.

One side of this new room had a long, high stationary shelf with three small half-windows above to give ample light. Beneath were shelves for glassware, both a dry and a steam sterilizer, an oil stove and other items. The home-made thermostat with its little kerosene lamp rested on a bracketed shelf next to his sink where he washed his glass. Of course the sink had no running water. A large pail and dipper nearby supplied this. The water had to be heated on the oil stove, and the sink drained through a lead pipe into another pail. The microscope, stains and boxes of slides stood on another table under the fourth and large window, and at its right was his shelf of books. The translation of the Koch paper was close at hand, dog-eared from repeated reference to its pages.

A solemn Irish patient named John Quinlan now watched over the thermostat, emptied the waste water, filled the other pail and cared for the experimental animals. In addition to tuberculosis, John suffered from a variety of ailments including epilepsy, so to Trudeau it was not surprising that he was so solemn. But he was a joy since he could do all the odd jobs and was faithful in looking after the animals. He grew more and more self-important and was skillful at discouraging curious patients who wandered into the laboratory.

On Trudeau's return from his morning calls one day, he found the long-awaited Dr. D'Avignon sitting in the parlor, smiling. "I took a look at your laboratory, doctor, or I tried to. That man in there refused to tell me a thing. I finally gave up and began to talk about the animals. What do you suppose he said when I asked him how they were getting on?"

" 'None of your business'?" Trudeau asked.

"No, he said, 'Well, they do do pretty well, sir, until the doctor begins to fool with them.' "

Trudeau laughed. "That about sums up the view of some of my famous medical colleagues."

The two physicians then went into the laboratory. John Quinlan retreated. After Trudeau explained his experiments, Dr. D'Avignon said, "I must be frank with you: I have little faith in your germ theory of tuberculosis; but would you be willing to take a little trouble to convince me?"

At first Trudeau was irritated, but he realized that his visitor must be open to conviction, at least. "What should I do?"

"As you know, there is a lot of tuberculosis up my way. I would like to send you several numbered samples of sputum. If you can tell me which ones come from patients with tuberculosis, I will believe everything you say." Although his voice was pleasant, his eyes showed serious doubt.

Trudeau had trouble suppressing a smile, for he knew that the shrewd little French-Canadian thought he had him trapped. "I will be glad to try the experiment."

When the five samples arrived, Trudeau made his usual tests. Only three of the containers held sputum showing tubercle bacilli.

He was surprised to see Dr. D'Avignon in Saranac a week later. The Frenchman brushed past John Quinlan's restraining arm, directly into the laboratory where he was working, test tubes in hand. D'Avignon smiled as proudly as if he had made the experiments himself. "You were exactly right, Dr. Trudeau, exactly! It's wonderful! Show me how to do that."

Happy as Trudeau was over this experience, his greatest satisfaction came during Dr. Loomis' next visit to the north woods. The New Yorker confessed that the experience with his Harvard student had convinced him. At last he, too, believed in germs!

XIII.

LANDMARKS

□□□

Dr. Loomis kept his promise. In the early summer of 1884 he wrote that he was sending two young factory girls as the first patients for the new sanatorium. They were too poor to pay their living costs, but one of the physician's friends had agreed to take over the charges for Alice and Mary Hunt. This would be three dollars a week for each girl—about half of the actual cost—the deficit to be made up through appeals to summer residents at St. Regis.

The Trudeaus drove their shaggy horse Kitty over to Saranac Lake to greet the girls. All during the trip he was excited and talkative. "How wonderful it will be, Lottie! We have at last made a beginning. I want to get these first patients on their feet by winter. I *must* succeed with them. It will do more than anything else to convince American doctors that proper care, fresh air and rest can arrest tuberculosis."

Lottie was unusually silent.

"Don't you agree?" he asked.

"Oh yes, wholeheartedly."

"Well then, why are you so serious? This is a joyous occasion, Lottie!"

"It's because I hate to see you build your hopes too high."

Trudeau tried to hide his irritation. "You can't blame me after all this planning. At last we have made a start."

He grew more and more excited as they ascended Mount Pisgah and drove onto the pasture. The plain, two-story frame building was beautiful to him, porchless and paintless though it was. While Lottie went inside to talk with Mrs. Norton, the farmer's wife, he stood looking at the house—the realization of all his hopes, at least in part. Then he walked along the bare slope among the jagged boulders and over to the zigzag fence that marked the old fox run. Once again his imagination painted the "Adirondack Cottage Sanitarium" of the future. He saw a completed administration building with a broad veranda, a dozen small, cozy cottages dotting a broad expanse of green lawn. He could see flower-bordered walks, lovely shade trees, gay, happy young people seated in lounging chairs singing and laughing, reading, pausing to admire the ever-shifting view as the clouds folded and unfolded among the mountaintops. He saw these patients gradually gaining strength, putting on weight, losing their hacking coughs, as the result of his rest treatment.

There would be visitors too, rich people eager to see for themselves the great wonders of the place, ready to give generously of their wealth. And physicians, dubious at first but easily converted to his ideas and ready to go back to their own communities to establish similar hospitals, to join in the fight against "The Great White Plague."

Trudeau was jolted out of his daydream by Lottie's excited voice: "Here they come!" He hurried toward her, along the slope.

There was Mr. Norton, one hand holding the reins, the other waving as a smile lit up his broad, ruddy face. Beside him were two girls huddled close together, with only their bare heads visible above the folds of a gray wool blanket. For a moment, as the farmer helped the girls to the ground, no one said a word. Trudeau stood fixed in his tracks. The new patients were painfully thin-faced and looked as if they were about to cry. One had a humped back.

Lottie was the first to regain her composure. "Welcome! I see that you are tired. That forty-mile ride from Ausable Forks is hard. I'm Mrs. Trudeau and this tall, balding, lanky man with the side-burns is your doctor."

As Trudeau came over to shake hands, Mrs. Norton and her two daughters rushed out of the house. Fortunately, they showed no surprise at the Hunt girls' bedraggled appearance, and after a moment of chatter the tension was gone. The new patients had more curiosity than worry in their faces now.

Mrs. Norton bustled around. "Now, M.J., you bring in their luggage. I want to get these tired girls to their room. I have coffee on the stove and some soup and a lovely roast . . ."

As she, her daughters and the Hunts entered the front door, Mr. Norton pulled a small wooden box from the back of his wagon. "Luggage? Why, doctor, they ain't got no luggage. This is for you, came from Merck's, it says on the box. The girls don't even have coats. I wrapped that blanket around them, but they shivered every foot of the way. Never said a solitary word."

The Trudeaus exchanged glances. Lottie said, "Yes, I'll go right down to our house and get warm clothes."

Trudeau was glad to be alone for a moment, to compose himself so that he could talk calmly with his patients, but his practiced eye told him only too well that the Hunt sisters were not what he needed to show the value of his experiment. With a heavy heart he entered the house.

During the next few hours he learned that the girls lived in a crowded tenement in lower New York. They had lost three sisters of consumption. Mary, the younger one, had tuberculosis of the spine, although the trouble in her lungs was not too extensive. Her sister Alice was very sick, with a heavy, almost constant cough. As he examined them, he kept wondering how Dr. Loomis could have made such a terrible mistake.

"I'm sure he understood that I wanted only those who have a chance to get well," he said to Lottie as they left for St. Regis.

"But the poor things. Isn't there some hope for them?"

"Very little."

"I don't understand, Eddie. If that's true, why did Dr. Loomis select the Hunt girls?"

He thought a moment, then answered: "My guess is that his kind heart got the better of his judgment. He's too good a chest man not to know they are advanced cases. Well, they are here. All we can do is to give them a chance."

That evening he wrote a carefully worded letter to Dr. Loomis:

Our purpose should be to supply a refuge for those patients who have a reasonable prospect of being restored to a life of usefulness. There are charities which offer to the consumptive a shelter wherein he may pass the last days of his life, but none holds out any hope of cure. Indeed, they shut their doors to all but the most advanced and hopeless cases. They avoid hospitalization of those who might live for a long period, since this would tie up beds needed for acute cases or for accidents. My plan is to supply a refuge for those who might be helped if offered early. No other institution offers this kind of service to people who cannot afford to defray all of their own costs. I admit that this is an experiment, but it is certainly well worth trying.

Dr. Loomis replied that he understood all this. In selecting the Hunt girls, sick though they were, he had to argue. Among the dozen patients he had examined, only they would go.

Trudeau's usual plan during the summer was to spend only one day a week at Saranac Lake, since he now had an extensive practice at St. Regis and there were many visitors at his Spitfire Lake camp. Dr. Luis Walton, Ed Harriman, now a rising young broker in New York, his Aspinwall cousins, and other friends came up for a few weeks. But the arrival of the Hunts complicated things. The girls had been at the sanatorium only three days when the Nortons sent word that he should come at once. Mrs. Norton met him at a side door.

"Doctor, I cannot do a thing with them. They stay in their room with all the windows shut tight, bundled to their eyebrows. They eat like mice. They will not drink milk. They cannot swallow the cod liver oil, and . . ."

Before the weary physician left an hour later, the Hunts were smiling, propped up in their beds wearing their robes, the warm breeze flowing into the room through wide-open windows. He had managed to get a pint of milk into each of them, as well as a large dose of cod liver oil.

"This was a good chance to send them back," he explained to Lottie. "They were homesick and willing to leave. But I just could not suggest it. When they feel stronger, perhaps—I do not know. I hate to think about it."

He felt better when the next patient arrived at Mount Pisgah. John O'Riley, twenty-five years old, had been ill for nine months. Although he had malaria as well as tuberculosis, Trudeau was confident that the young man had a good chance for recovery. He was naturally cheerful, ready to do exactly as he was told. He listened as Trudeau told him to walk slowly, "never stand when you can sit, never sit when you can lie, eat everything we give you."

A simple prescription perhaps, but one which is still a valuable piece of advice any sufferer from active tuberculosis can follow. At this period there were no surgical techniques, no X ray, no chemotherapy, to aid in the treatment of tuberculosis. Nor was the removal of a lung or a part of it thought possible. Trudeau had read about one surgical technique called aspiration, used in England and Europe. The surgeon made an incision and drew off a fluid that sometimes filled the pleural cavity, in order to relieve pressure on the lung and heart and permit more normal breathing, but this was a rarely needed technique. In 1850 Dr. Henry I. Bowditch, a noted Bostonian practitioner, improved on this idea. He and his co-worker, a surgeon named Morrill Wyman, developed a trocar, a long, hollow, pointed instrument open at both ends, to be pushed into the cavity to tap off the fluid. Since the trocar was very small, it did away with the necessity for an incision.

Trudeau had not performed this simple operation but kept a trocar in his bag in case of an emergency, which came fairly often in later years when his practice was very large. On his day-to-day rounds, however, he always insisted that complete rest was essential, and O'Riley followed the advice religiously. Within a month he gained five pounds and had a normal temperature.

Other patients arrived during this summer—all through Dr. Loomis. But it was now apparent that willing and eager as the Norton family was, they could not handle all of the work or the patients. Some of the newcomers complained about the routine, insisting that they simply could not rest all day. A few of them did not know how to read. How were they to pass the long hours? When one of the patients had a hemorrhage, the Norton girls rushed out of the room, screaming and causing general panic. Again Trudeau had to calm everyone and instruct Mrs. Norton in the handling of emergencies. Then he hired a woman to care for the female patients and a retired guide to take care of the sicker men.

Meanwhile, work proceeded on the first cottage. "The Little Red," as it became known after it received its first coat of barn paint, was a small one-room building with space for two beds, two washstands, a stove and a couple of chairs. The small front veranda held only one lounging chair, but this was sufficient since Trudeau was still having trouble with patients who were afraid of fresh air.

The Little Red was completed in February, 1885, the first cottage of its kind in the world. It became a shrine to thousands of Americans who followed Trudeau's rest cure and lived to boast about it. The doctor himself considered it a symbol of all his aims, his hopes, his dreams.

Dr. Loomis still had difficulty in finding enough patients, and

Trudeau wondered whether he would be able to fill the beds in the two new cottages that would be started in the spring. Loomis said that other physicians were reluctant to refer patients. But when the Hunt girls returned to New York much improved and O'Riley was able to return to his job as a hatter, the picture changed somewhat. During the summer of 1885 each mail brought questions about the sanatorium. Few applications came through physicians, however. The sufferers often arrived unannounced, very ill, on stretchers, on horseback and, in one case, by foot.

At the end of one particular hard, snowy day in late autumn, Trudeau came into his office at Saranac Lake to find a poorly dressed man waiting for him. At first he thought he was looking at a tramp ready for a handout. "Who are you?"

The thin, hollow-eyed stranger arose. "Be you Dr. Trudeau?"

"What can I do for you?" He scarcely looked at the man.

The stranger sat down again and shoved his hands into his ragged jacket pockets. "Well now, you don't look none like a doctor. I would've said you was one of them bicycle fellows like I seed in New York."

Trudeau wore his usual outfit—heavy pants stuffed into long woolen socks and his hunter's cap. "Well, what's the matter with you?"

The man looked at him, open-mouthed. "What's the matter, you say? Why, if you had half an eye you could see that I'm almost dead with the consumption!"

Trudeau sat down, crossed his long, thin legs and stared. That was a blunt truth. The man's drawn face, the bright red spots on his cheekbones, his hunched, thin shoulders, the tired eyes . . . "Tell me about it then. Where did you come from?"

"Well, the doctors put me in a big hospital ward in Brooklyn. But I looked around me and sized things up a bit. I ain't no fool no matter how I look." He narrowed his eyes and peered at Trudeau. "There was about fifty sick blokes in that there ward, and I wasn't there but three days when I seed some of them carried out foot-first. I says to myself, this is going to happen to me if I do not get out of this place. So I lit out."

Trudeau managed to ask, "What made you come up here?"

"I heard one of them sick ones tell about you and Saranac Lake. I made up my mind that I would strike out. I hadn't a cent and was pretty weak, but I begged enough to pay my fare to Yonkers. When I got there, I moseyed down the street and rung every doorbell. I begged cold victuals. But by the time my stomach was full I was rounded up. They put me in jail."

Here the tramp broke out laughing. He coughed hard for a moment, then continued his story. "They looked me over, I guess, and made up their minds I was like as not to die on their hands. Thought it was cheaper to buy me a ticket to the next place and let me die there. This kept up till I got to Ausable Forks. I hoofed it from there. Now, what can you do for me, doctor?"

Trudeau did not doubt the man's story for a moment. What could he do for him? Kitty, hitched to the cutter, was still at the door. "I'll take you to a little boardinghouse down the street."

As they climbed in, he asked, "What has brought you to this bad condition—drink?"

"Oh no. Not drink. It don't agree with me."

Trudeau was amused by this observation. When he examined the man the next day, he discovered that he was one of those old chronic cases which would never be cured but might carry on for years, if he lived a moderate life. He was surprised to find that the tramp's sputum contained no bacillus, and when the man insisted that he try to support himself, Trudeau asked a general handyman to build a rough-board shanty on a vacant lot. The tramp slept on a straw bed there during the spring and summer, and the Berkeley Hotel nearby furnished him left-over food. During the day he sold fruit to passers-by. He never complained while he was in Saranac, and Trudeau often took him along when he had to make night calls in the country. The man gained strength and weight and seemed perfectly happy until one day he casually remarked, "This winter here is too cold for me. I like the South."

Trudeau gave no thought to this remark until the tramp disappeared one night.

When townspeople asked about the strange patient, he always

said, "Oh, he went South for the winter." But he often wondered about him and wished that physicians were as willing to experiment with the open-air life as that tramp had been. Dr. Loomis was doing his best to convert the medical men in New York, but none showed enough curiosity even to visit the Adirondack Cottage Sanitarium.

Trudeau finally came up with an idea. He would try his theories on rabbits—and show the value of environment through a scientific experiment. There was a small island opposite his camp on Spitfire Lake, ideal for his purpose. There he inoculated five rabbits with pure cultures of tubercle bacilli and allowed them to run at will on the sunny island. He placed his second lot of inoculated animals in a dark, damp cave. Five others—not inoculated—lived in another cave. By the end of a summer the rabbits he had inoculated and kept in a cave had died of tuberculosis, according to the autopsies. The other cave dwellers were emaciated but alive. Later the autopsies showed no tuberculosis. Of the inoculated rabbits permitted to run free on the island, all but one had recovered from the disease.

Dr. Loomis was not slow to see the importance of these dramatic results. "Now, how can we summarize this, say, in one sentence?"

"Well, we can point out that bad surroundings alone do not cause tuberculosis, but once the germs are in the body, the course of the disease is greatly influenced by environment."

"Fine! Absolute proof!" Dr. Loomis clapped his knees to emphasize his enthusiasm.

He returned to Trudeau's camp the next day. "I've entered your name for membership in two societies—the American Climatological Association and the Association of American Physicians. You'll be elected to both."

Loomis then urged him to write a paper on the Bunny Island experiments for presentation at the next meeting of the Climatological Association in Baltimore the following May.

Trudeau had never attended a national medical meeting, and the proposal that he read a paper frightened him, but he realized that it was an opportunity and could go a long way in winning over the conservatives in the medical fraternity.

It was unusually hot when he and Lottie arrived in New York that spring, and hotter still in Baltimore as he and Dr. Loomis stepped off the train. His hotel room was stifling and although he tried to relax, he could not. By morning he was as tired as when he went to bed. He could not eat a bite of breakfast—the sight and smell of the bacon and eggs nauseated him.

Dr. Loomis remarked that it might be due to the sudden change in climate, the humidity in Baltimore, but urged him to eat. By this time Trudeau knew that he was very nervous over what would happen at the meeting when he read his paper, but he did not explain this to Loomis.

The large hall was packed as they took their seats near the back. Trudeau tried to listen to the papers—they were all a meaningless jumble. The platform looked very large and high. What if he stumbled on his way to the rostrum? He counted the steps. Four. Yes, there was a reading stand. His hands were already so shaky that he could not possibly read if he had to hold his paper. His paper . . . How would these men receive it? With indifference. He tried to judge the applause after the finish of each paper. The few comments that followed were humdrum. Only one was greeted with enthusiasm. Several men walked out during the next reading; he could hear their voices in the hall. They were laughing.

Dr. Loomis nudged him. "You're next."

Trudeau's right hand touched his coat pocket. He started to rise. He felt dizzy and faint. Leaning over to Dr. Loomis, he managed to whisper, "I feel sick."

His friend took one look at him and said, "Get up and go out in the hall."

Trudeau finally managed to get to his feet. He was conscious of a low murmur of voices as he started up the aisle. Then everything went black.

The next thing he knew, he was lying on the floor just outside the meeting room. Before he opened his eyes he heard the voice of Dr. Loomis: "Where is your paper?"

Trudeau pointed to his pocket. He was too weak to move his head or legs.

"Just lie there until you feel better," a strange voice said.

"Try these smelling salts again," said another.

Then once more there was the voice of Dr. Loomis, strong but at a distance. He was reading the paper. Trudeau listened. Were the points perfectly clear? Dr. Loomis was doing very well since he had no chance to look at the paper before he went to the platform. What must those men think of him, unable to read his own paper . . . It was too long. There, Loomis was coming to the end of it. Trudeau held his breath and waited.

" 'A consideration of the evidence teaches that though environment may bear but the relation of a predisposing cause to microbic infection, it is, nevertheless, a potent factor in determining the future type and even the final results of the disease, and that if we may not underestimate the pathogenic properties of the bacillus, the effects of extremes of environment on the resisting power of the cells of the body as an element in this complex problem which should not be ignored.' "

There was a moment of silence, then Loomis said, "It seems to me that this is one of the most valuable and carefully prepared papers that we have had before this society. It gives definite shape to our clinical observations."

A burst of applause followed these remarks. Trudeau could not decide whether it was the loudest he had heard, but it reassured him as he lay there in the hall. In another moment he saw men rushing toward him, smiling, talking, reaching for his hands.

"A fine paper!"

"Never heard a more lucid presentation."

"That was good!"

"Are you feeling better?"

For the first time Trudeau noticed how hard the floor was. He lifted himself to his elbows, then with the help of several men arose and walked slowly into the street. "Yes, I feel much better. But I am thoroughly disgusted with myself!"

"I told you to eat your breakfast," Loomis said. "You must not skip meals just because of the heat."

Trudeau could not keep from smiling. Loomis sounded as if he were scolding a stubborn patient. "It was not due to the heat, doctor. I had a bad case of stage fright. My stomach was full of butterflies."

A small, rather portly man, with bright eyes shining from under drooping lids, patted him on the back. "Shame on you! Anyone who can do that kind of research and present it so well ought to be able to read his own paper."

The speaker was Dr. William Osler, one of the founders of the Johns Hopkins Medical School. A few minutes later he introduced his colleague, Dr. William Welch, also a famous physician and teacher at the school who had worked in the Koch laboratory; he, too, expressed his enthusiasm over the paper.

Suddenly Trudeau realized that he was no longer nervous. He forgot about his stage fright and the heat and listened with rapt attention and gratitude as these eminent men praised his work, asked questions about his theories, his hopes and his troubles. He was especially happy about Osler's interest, since this Canadian-born physician, trained at McGill University, was well versed in the latest developments in all fields of clinical medicine. Osler's lack of professional jealousy, his willingness to speak up in praise of young doctors and his courage had won for him a pre-eminent reputation in the medical profession.

Trudeau thought of Lottie and how pleased she would be to learn of this interest in his experiments and the sanatorium.

As he was about to say good-by to the group of men, a tall, distinguished-looking physician joined them. Dr. Loomis introduced Vincent Bowditch of Boston: "The son of Henry Ingersoll Bowditch, whose writings you know."

The newcomer spoke, a look of eagerness in his eyes. "The men in the hall are waiting for you to return, Dr. Trudeau. They insist that you come to the platform. Your paper created a sensation!"

Dr. Osler looked up into Bowditch's face and said, "If he feels equal to it. He fainted, you know." Then he turned to Trudeau: "How about it?"

Trudeau managed a smile, although he now felt very close to tears. He shook his head. "I—uh—that is, the air is too close in the auditorium. I am most grateful, but . . ." He could say no more.

A few hours later he confessed to Loomis that he had not over-come his stage fright and feared that if he had gone back he might have fainted again.

"A shame in a way," his friend replied, patting him on the shoulder. "I heard a few minutes ago that some of the men were planning a kind of celebration for you this evening!"

Trudeau did not try to hide his happiness, his gratitude. He smiled through his tears and shook his head. "This has all been too much, doctor. I must leave Baltimore in the morning. I just did not expect them to take my work this seriously."

Loomis laughed. "Well, no harm done. Your modesty will only increase your reputation. You will get used to reading papers. The next one will be no chore at all."

Trudeau did not reply. The mere thought of reading another paper brought butterflies to his stomach and made him dizzy. "I will never read another paper at a medical meeting," he told himself. "I am not equal to it. I can hardly wait to get home.

He and Lottie returned to Saranac the next day. This home-com-ing was different from any of the previous ones. As he walked into his laboratory, he knew that he was no longer a wilderness physician holding out a weak, lone hand to poor city sufferers. Other physi-cians had joined in the crusade.

XIV.

THE SPREADING GOSPEL

Trudeau was deeply conscious of his debt to those who gave money for his sanatorium, and his first annual report was to serve as a plea for continued support. So far, he had spent fourteen thousand dollars on an experiment without precedent in this country. "And those who had assumed the responsibility were totally inexperienced

in such work," he said. "The management has been beset by diffi-
culties. The results obtained have led us to hope that the experiment
may fairly be said to have proved a success."

Twenty-six patients were admitted during the two and a half
years. While two of them died and four, including the Hunt sisters,
showed little or no lasting improvement, fourteen returned to their
jobs, apparently restored to health. Eight were still under treatment.

His report for 1887 was more confident. He had paid all of the
expenses with cash on hand and the bed capacity was increased by
more than one-third. No one died at the sanatorium that year.
Twenty-two of the forty patients were able to return home. "Four
have been cured," he said.

As time went on, he used the word "cure" less frequently, substi-
tuting the more cautious and realistic term, "arrested case."

As Mr. Riddle had predicted, growth brought increased financial
trouble. While wealthy friends continued to make up the annual
deficit, more patients meant more salaries, a laundry was needed, a
safe and adequate water supply, and a good sewerage system. They
could no longer depend on runoff to provide water for cleaning and
washing. Even the addition of a cistern was insufficient. Then there
was the problem of what to do with patients who were well enough
to leave the sanatorium but still too weak to return to their old jobs.
Ways had to be found to offer them employment and shelter. Even
when they were able to go home, many of them preferred to remain
in Saranac Lake. A large number of former patients had suffered
setbacks upon their return to city life, and such reports made others
overcautious at times.

Trudeau was amazed to discover this reluctance to go home even
after their "cures" were apparently well-established. It was more
than the beauty and climate of Saranac Lake that kept them there.
They had come to look on him as a father to whom they could
always turn for help or comfort.

His early difficulty in finding patients in the first stages of tuberculosis was at an end, except for those referred by physicians lack-
ing in the skill necessary to detect the early stages of the disease.
He could not bear to turn sick people away from his door, even

when he could not give them beds at the sanatorium. He either took money out of his own pocket or begged it from one of his friends so they might stay at a boarding home. He now had a long waiting list at the sanatorium in spite of the increased charge to five dollars a week.

When he complained to Dr. Loomis about his burden of constant begging, the fear that he would not be able to meet his annual deficit, the New Yorker said, "I told you so. Must you always take poor people? You can demonstrate the value of the treatment with the rich just as easily."

Trudeau could not hide his annoyance. "Let someone else do that. I want to stop the spread of this disease as much as I can. It spreads fastest among the poor—in the tenements. Many of them take it to their offices and factories and pass it on to others."

Trudeau had the uneasy feeling that those who contributed to the sanatorium did so out of friendship rather than through conviction that his idea was sound. On some days he was so discouraged that he would say to Lottie, "I feel like blowing up the sanatorium and laboratory."

He noticed that when he said this, Fitz usually arrived a short time later with the suggestion that they go out for a long hunt, and knew that his wife had sent for him. Trudeau returned from these expeditions rested and hopeful again. But he never voiced anything but hope to visitors who now came in increasing numbers to Saranac. "These patients can be saved, unless they contract pneumonia or fall out of bed," he always told them. "My cottage plan is ideal. You noticed how cheerful those girls in Little Red were?"

The visitors always said yes to this question.

"Their minds are at rest. They have no money worries. I hope to have more cottages. Have you seen the rows of beds at Bellevue?"

At this point he again turned his visitor's attention to what Lottie called his tear-jerker stories, such as the one about a lovely young woman who had a fine chance for recovery *if* some kindhearted person would pay for her care. All this took time and energy, but it was a hardhearted man who could resist his dramatic pleas. Few did.

"The old skinflint!" he would say when this happened. "Maybe I did not make it strong enough."

Although Trudeau still looked back on his Baltimore experience with a mixture of horror and dismay, it paid big dividends. Dr. Osler, Dr. Welch and their colleagues at Johns Hopkins were spreading his gospel. They accepted with glowing thanks the periodic shipments of tubercle-bacilli cultures which he sent for use in their laboratory. Dr. Prudden and Dr. Hodenpyl continued their interest too; and whenever he went to New York to solicit funds for the sanatorium, he always saved time for a period of work in their old room. Each time he returned to Saranac refreshed and stimulated.

He plunged into his research again, repeating his work with rabbits on Bunny Island and adding refinements to his theories on environment. His conservatism as a scientist was in striking contrast to his work as a promoter who allowed his enthusiasm to carry him into the clouds when he talked about his sanatorium.

The town now had a world-wide reputation as the leading resort for the tuberculous, and several of the more wealthy patients built their own homes there. One of these was George Cooper of New York, nephew of the famous Peter Cooper and a highly-intelligent patient. Through Cooper's generosity the problems of drinking water and drainage were solved. He and his sister Julia donated money for cottages as well. But the finest addition to the colony of health-seekers during the early years was a former medical student from Johns Hopkins, referred by Dr. Welch who agreed to pay the young man's expenses.

Frank Ingersoll had neither money nor family. After Trudeau examined him he knew that Welch was correct. Here was an advanced case. "I'm sorry that we did not discover your case earlier," he said.

"You mean I must leave?"

"Oh no," Trudeau replied hastily. "I'll find a boardinghouse for you. We'll do our best."

"A boardinghouse? But I want to live at the sanatorium. That's why I came." The young man's voice was excited and shrill.

Trudeau sighed. He could not justify such a move to his supporters. "You're very sick. Didn't Dr. Welch explain our policy?"

Ingersoll's face went blank. "I know my condition. I don't expect you to work a miracle—but, doctor, I am a third-year medical student. I see no reason to accept charity."

He arose, walked to the door leading to the laboratory and waved his thin arm toward the bottles and test tubes. "Perhaps I could help in there—wash glass, keep up the fires. My hope was that I could help at the sanatorium. It would make up in a way for having to leave school."

As Trudeau watched the honest, pleading face, the intense, burning eyes, he felt strangely humble. "I understand."

That night, after Frank Ingersoll was settled in his small room in the administration building, Trudeau tried to explain to Lottie what his experience that day meant: "The boy is doomed, doomed! And yet I don't feel sorry for him. I envy Frank Ingersoll."

"Envy? How?"

"I wish I had his courage."

As the weeks passed, he began to wonder how he had managed to get along without the help of this former student. Ingersoll seemed to have but one purpose—to cheer, educate and encourage the patients, to help them, through rest, back to full health—a goal he could never achieve for himself. Trudeau almost forgot that his new assistant was gradually losing ground. He was always smiling, patient with the complainers, teaching them to live with their handicaps, to accept the realities of their future, to believe that a half-loaf was better than no loaf at all.

The small world of Saranac Lake saw other additions in 1887. The Trudeaus learned that a new baby was on the way. Francis, named for Trudeau's brother, arrived amid fear that he would be a disrupting influence in the well-established routine of his family's life, but he won their hearts immediately, and soon they were congratulating themselves.

Only seventeen-year-old Chatte complained. "Why do I have to go away to school this year? Francis is so sweet. Can't I stay and help take care of him?"

"Now, dear," Lottie said, "Ann Gaffney and I can manage quite well. Your father and I believe that it would be best for you to go to New York for a year or two."

Trudeau tried to sound cheerful. "You owe it to yourself to get more schooling. You know very little beyond sledding, swimming and rowing."

The house was lonely after Chatte left. Both parents missed her lively, smiling ways, and even Ned complained that it was too bad his sister had to "get finished" so far from home.

Soon after her departure Trudeau received a letter from the great English writer, Robert Louis Stevenson, telling him that a physician in Edinburgh suggested that he spend the following winter in Saranac and put himself in Trudeau's care. Stevenson's arrival in the United States created a sensation in New York. Reporters filed long stories about the colorful, appealing man, and Trudeau was by now too shrewd a promoter to lose sight of the publicity value Stevenson would offer Saranac Lake.

The town was in a state of high expectation when the famous author arrived to live in the Baker cottage at the edge of town. No one had seen such excitement since the days when Ralph Waldo Emerson and James Russell Lowell came to the village on their way to "The Philosopher's Camp," years before. These authors had also stayed for a time at the Bakers' house.

Trudeau was the first to call on Mr. Stevenson. When he finished his examination, he said, "Your case is quiet. Very little chance for me to do anything spectacular for you—unfortunately. You may put on your shirt now."

The tall, lean-faced author stroked his long mustache and with an amused look said, "Thank goodness you have finished pounding my chest. That was the longest fifteen minutes I ever lived through."

Trudeau was puzzled for an instant, until he saw Stevenson reaching for a cigarette. "Oh well, I cannot examine a man while he's smoking," he said impatiently. While he did not forbid smoking, he discouraged it in patients who coughed as likely to irritate their lung tissues.

The two men sat in front of the brick fireplace for an hour. "Actually, you have no need for my services," Trudeau confessed.

"That's good. I really came up here out of curiosity. That and to get away from people." Stevenson rose and put his cigarette on the mantel edge.

Trudeau glanced up. "If you came here to escape people, you made a sad mistake. My wife says that everyone is begging for a chance to meet and entertain you."

"Entertain?" Stevenson almost shouted. "What an awful bore!"

Eddie thought it best to change the subject. Since he had never been a great lover of literature, he decided to tell his patient about the work at the sanatorium and something of his laboratory experiments.

The author listened attentively enough, but during a pause he suddenly turned and said, "I understand from Mrs. Baker that you are religious. How can a scientist, a physician, go through the motions? She says you are a pillar of the Episcopal Church!"

Trudeau did not know how to reply to this peculiar remark. "Perhaps I am. What's wrong with that? I don't see the point."

Stevenson lit another cigarette and paced up and down the small room. "Do you mean to sit there and tell me that a man with your training and brains can take stock in all that folderol? Religion is for the uneducated, the superstitious. Intelligent men? No!"

For a moment Trudeau was at a loss for words. Then his temper rose. "You amaze me! It's true that my life is bound up in the study and practice of medicine, with the facts of life and death. Religion is something above and beyond mere experiments."

"Then you do believe in all those myths? Now, I have all the respect in the world for a man like you. I even admit that doctors are often very great idealists. That is something I understand. You express your finer impulses through your skill in healing. I do it with my pen. But all this talk about immortality, about a higher being? How do you explain that?"

"I do not even try." Trudeau had trouble keeping his voice under control. "You cannot explain or test religion by scientific standards. My experiences—watching the ill fight courageous battles—these are proof enough. You cannot explain religion any more than you can explain love. When you see patients meet death with a smile, you feel humble. At such times man can, if he will, feel very close to God. He must have faith when he sits with a young man close to eternity. Otherwise all suffering is senseless, healing too."

Trudeau was tempted to bring Frank Ingersoll to the Baker cottage, but he did not. His assistant had neither time nor strength to waste on a person who left religion out of his world.

As the winter passed, Trudeau found that Stevenson was a man of fine character, a religious man in practice, if not in belief. As long as he kept his illustrious patient off the forbidden subject, they had good times together. Frequently, after a hard day or work at the sanatorium or in his laboratory, he would drive old Kitty out to Baker's and spend a pleasant hour with Stevenson, arguing about trifles such as the virtues of American and British systems of handling baggage. He gave up all attempts to discuss his work, for Stevenson shuddered at the mere mention of stark, unpleasant facts.

Naturally the Trudeaus looked forward to letters from Chatte. They came often at first, full of talk about her new school friends, sandwiched between expressions of homesickness and the usual statement that she hoped this year would end her "exile." Neither parent took her complaints seriously. Perhaps she had been kept too close, too much with the family. Then in January both Ed Harriman and Minnie Aspinwall wrote that Chatte was not looking well. Her appetite was gone and she complained of indigestion. Still, her parents assured each other, "It is the strangeness. She is not used to being cooped up in the city.

Finally Trudeau grew suspicious and fearful. "Tell Chatte to come home at Eastertime, Lottie." It was so unlike her to be ill, but he said nothing about his fears.

It was a great relief when the holiday arrived. Now he would be able to see for himself. He arranged to meet his daughter alone at the new railroad station, the recently completed extension of the line from Ausable Forks to Saranac Lake.

When Chatte stepped from the train, he groaned. Of course she was smiling, but instead of a plump, healthy young girl, she was now pale, thin. All the way to the house he watched her, trying to calm his fears.

While Lottie took her upstairs to her room to chat a while, Trudeau went into the office and closed the door. He recalled, as if it were only yesterday, that afternoon in Newport when Frank came to him, so ill. The same old story. She must have inherited a predisposition which she could not overcome in spite of her outdoor life, her outwardly sturdy frame, her active interest in sports. For the first time Chatte had been living in a city, spending most of her time cooped up in school, in a dormitory with other girls. The radical change may have been responsible. The strain of living away from Saranac, the homesickness were a drain on the child. She had not coughed so far, so perhaps her mother did not suspect. What should he do? Perhaps he only imagined the worst. He decided to say nothing until he could make sure.

When Francis was put to bed and the family sat down to dinner, Trudeau forced himself to smile with the others. He was relieved that everything was normal—Lottie dispelling arguments—everything, except the lump in his own throat and the full, unreal sensation at the pit of his stomach. Out of the side of his eye he watched his daughter peck at her food with too-quick, nervous hands. He tried to assure himself that the drawn lines around her mouth were the result of the long train trip.

"Oh, it is such a relief to be home!" Chatte said as she rested her chin in the palm of her right hand.

"Is that why you let me eat the chicken breast?" Ned asked.

A bit of the old gleam returned to Chatte's black eyes. "No, just my generous soul."

As soon as the meal was over, Trudeau stole up the back stairs into her room. He found what he was looking for—her handkerchief, in a small wad on her dresser. Quickly he put it in his pocket and tiptoed down to his laboratory. John Quinlan was stoking the fire.

"Working again tonight, doctor?"

As soon as his helper left, Trudeau quietly turned the lock on his laboratory door and ran his test. The results were positive! Worse still, the bacilli count was rather high. For a minute he stood in front of his microscope staring through the lens at the bunched rods on the slide. Then without stopping to put on his coat or cap, he walked through the office and stepped outside. He stumbled along to the stable where Kitty stood munching the hay which Quinlan had tossed into the manger. As he stroked her rough coat, he poured out his anguish, a volley of angry words followed by quiet tears. When last he was able to compose himself he returned to the house to break the news to Lottie.

After a few minutes of shocked silence she said, "Don't worry too much, dear. Chatte has always been so strong—until now. Where is your usual optimism? We'll pull her through this ordeal."

Optimism? The bacilli count meant one thing to Edward Livingston Trudeau: his daughter had more than a minimal case of tuberculosis. Her naturally cheerful temperament might help, and rest, good food and care would prolong her life. But there was no use in fooling himself with false hope. Chatte was a very sick girl.

XV.

FALSE CURES

Trudeau could detect little outward change in Chatte's condition during the first weeks after her return from New York, but his optimism failed completely each time he examined her chest or listened to her frequent nighttime cough. Unable to sleep, he often arose in the early morning hours to work in his laboratory, hoping that he would somehow turn a miracle, find a way to conquer the bacillus that now threatened the life of his only daughter.

Since the time of Lister, research had been aimed at the finding of antiseptics that would kill germs on contact. Researchers in the field of tuberculosis were busy trying, then discarding one new product after another. While Trudeau was still in medical school he had read about the work of a French scientist named Bastien who advocated the use of hydrofluoric acid vapor for the treatment of phthisis. His theory came as the result of his observations in Baccarat glass factories where tuberculous workers, using the acid to etch their designs, appeared to improve in health. The mild flurry of optimism created by Bastien's announcement soon died out, and little was heard about it until September, 1887, when William Thompson of Manchester, England, reported that he, too, found hydrofluoric acid beneficial. Others came forward with similar claims.

When Trudeau read of these new claims he decided to make his own experiments. It was a result of his feeling of desperation, since he had already tried various antiseptics such as creosote and carbolic acid without the slightest success. His first experiment was with direct injections of acid-treated bacilli in rabbits.

His son Ned, now a tall, handsome lad of fifteen and keenly interested in the work, went out with Fitz and after an afternoon in the hills brought fourteen healthy animals to the pen near the house.

As soon as the family finished dinner, Trudeau set to work and as usual these days had to shoo Ned out of the laboratory.

"Aw, I'd much rather help inoculate rabbits than study that old science textbook," the boy complained.

"When you know everything in that book, son, you'll be ready to try a few experiments on your own. I have too much at stake to explain as I'd have to for you. Understand?"

A wan smile crossed his son's face as his glance shifted from Trudeau's tired, anxious eyes. "Yes, I understand."

There was no telling about a boy this age. Ned's interest might be only transitory or it might increase with the years. Trudeau hoped that it would grow, but he thought it best to hold a tight rein on the boy rather than risk his becoming weary of the long, tedious experiments which he could not, as yet, really comprehend. Handling a chemical as volatile, corrosive and caustic as hydrofluoric acid was dangerous for the uninitiated. Now, as he listened to Ned's heavy steps on the stairs, his heart grew a bit lighter.

He worked all evening, inoculating two control rabbits with fresh cultures of tubercle bacillus, then preparing five watch glasses which he filled with solutions of acid, varying in strength from very weak to very strong. He added equal amounts of tubercle bacilli to each solution, inoculated twelve other rabbits with mixtures taken from the glasses and returned them to the pen with the controls.

It was a matter of waiting now, so Trudeau went to bed. He was too tired and much too nervous to fall asleep, but as he lay down and pulled the covers around his chin, he thought of his standard advice to the patients—"Never stand when you can sit, never sit when you can lie." Well, if he could not sleep, he could at least stay horizontal.

Chatte was coughing again . . .

Within two weeks the control rabbits died, and autopsy showed the usual extensive tuberculous lesions. Several days later the rabbits he had inoculated with weak mixtures of acid solution and bacilli also died, and their autopsies showed extensive tuberculosis. The ten others were still alive two months later.

The conclusions? Evidently it required very strong doses of acid to affect the bacilli at all.

Now it was time to try inhalations of hydrofluoric acid vapor. The vapor proved as harmless to the germs in rabbit lungs as if it were pure mountain air. Fearing that someone might claim that inhalations were effective in humans if not in rabbits, he selected a group of patients who had only moderately advanced cases of tuberculosis and asked them if they wanted to submit to the tests.

He chose an especially eager young man as his first "guinea pig," led him to a very small room that had been made as airtight as possible, and asked him to sit there for an hour. Nearby was a lead crucible with hydrofluoric acid in it, set over a pan of hot water heated by a small alcohol lamp. "Now, just breathe normally," he said to the patient. "If you find that the vapors irritate your bronchial tubes, give me a signal at once."

The young man seemed to look on the experiment as a lark. "As you say, doctor," he said with a broad smile.

As Trudeau watched through the door window, he saw the vapor gradually filling the small room. Finally the haze was so thick that he could barely see through the glass. After an hour the patient was still sitting there, arms crossed, inhaling the vapor. When Trudeau opened the door and window and told him he could leave, the young man said, "That stuff tickled my nose. Kind of funny sensation."

After several months of experiments with this and other patients, Trudeau reported to Lottie, "Might as well have kept the window open—except for one thing."

"What is that?"

"Well, our good mountain air would not have etched the windows. They are thoroughly frosted."

Lottie looked around. "Did the vapor etch the patients too? My goodness, Eddie, that is awful."

Trudeau quieted her fears. As far as he could tell, the effort and time was a total loss. He had nothing further to add to his experiments with hydrofluoric acid. The time had come to write his report for the New York *Medical News*.

His next experiment was with hot-air inhalations—another highly touted "cure." Three patients who had been ill less than a year, with minor lesions, took the treatment for one to four hours daily in the small room. After three months he noticed that the first two improved slightly. The third patient showed no effect whatsoever. Was the result in the first two due to the inhalations or only a natural development attendant on the "rest cure"? A fourth patient was a former clerk, twenty-three years old with no tuberculosis history in his family. He had a temperature of 101 degrees when he entered the sanatorium in February, 1889, and reported that he had been ill since the previous July, when he began to lose weight. In spite of the hot-air inhalations he was gradually getting worse.

Trudeau's report on these experiments appeared in a September issue, 1889, of *Medical News*:

We draw two conclusions from these cases. The therapeutic value of hot air inhalations is doubtful. They were not able to prevent growth or diminish the virulence of microbes in the body. Even if either hydrofluoric acid or hot air killed germs on contact, they could not reach those imbedded in lung tissues.

He was back where he started—the only known treatment that meant anything at all was good food, rest, pleasant environment, freedom from worry and fresh air. It was most discouraging. Sometimes, after a long day at the sanatorium, examining patients, encouraging the despondent ones, listening to the lively chatter among the less ill who sat bundled up on the veranda, he felt that he simply had to give up his experiments for the time being. He was getting close to fifty, now, balding, thin-faced and so weary that even his patients remarked on it. But thoughts of eager faces, of Chatte, spurred him on, often far into the night.

He must find some other line for investigation.

A short time after he published the article on hot-air inhalations, he received a letter from young Dr. Vincent Bowditch, the son of the physician who invented the trocar technique for removing fluid from the chest cavity. This promising young Bostonian, whom he had met in Baltimore, announced that he was coming to Saranac for a visit. Trudeau was very happy about this, for it was a rare occasion. Few doctors took the trouble to come all the way to Saranac Lake from points as distant as Boston. He met his visitor at the train, and before he had a chance to say hello, Bowditch called, "Well, I have come for help!"

Trudeau, who supposed that the man had come to talk over his articles, laughed aloud. "Well, sir, you have come to the wrong man. I need help myself!"

Bowditch threw his traveling bag in the back of the cutter, and as he climbed into the front seat he said, "I say, you look as if you are going hunting. I'm not up here to shoot squirrels."

Trudeau was embarrassed. Indeed, he was a striking contrast to this handsome, nattily dressed young physician. He wore his leggings and turtle-neck sweater with his hunting cap pulled down over his ears. While his patients had long ago grown accustomed to this costume, he knew that no city doctor would dream of going around in this fashion. "Well, I live in these clothes. You're out in the sticks, Dr. Bowditch. I'll rustle up leggings for you, if you'd like."

Bowditch smiled and shook his head. "Won't be necessary. Can't stay long. I just want to cry on your shoulder, if you don't mind.

You see, I had a little bout with this bacillus myself. While I came through all right, it set me to thinking. I hope to open a small sanatorium in Massachusetts."

Trudeau was all attention now. He forgot his self-consciousness, his depressed spirits. The visit took on a new aspect. "You will? That's the best news I've had in months. Why, it's wonderful! The gospel is spreading!"

"Hold on a minute. I said I *expect* to open a sanatorium. There's plenty of opposition to the idea. Some of my medical colleagues are dashing cold water on the enterprise. When I speak about it, they say, 'I don't believe in segregating consumptives. That must be depressing for them.' Now, how do I get around that?"

Trudeau immediately pulled on the reins. Instead of allowing Kitty to turn into his driveway, he steered to the left and they began the long ride up the slope of Mount Pisgah. "So that's what they say, is it?" he asked in a sarcastic tone. "Come along with me and I'll show you how to get around that criticism. It's ridiculous!"

It was disgusting. Why didn't these critics take the trouble to come to Saranac and see for themselves? Why were they so bullheaded? Why was it that the majority of physicians who had come to see the light were men who themselves had suffered from tuberculosis? When they pulled up in front of the administration building, Trudeau hopped out and motioned to his visitor. "Look up there on the veranda," he said in a triumphant tone. "See those smiling faces. Hear their laughter?"

A small group of young men were singing to the music of a banjo, while several girls near them giggled and applauded enthusiastically.

A smile came over Bodwitch's face. "Too bad I can't bottle that music and laughter. I'd sure like to take it back to Boston with me."

After a tour of the cottages and main building, Trudeau led the visitor into his private office. "You saw how cheerful they all looked —except for the two in Little Red. They are new, homesick. It is astonishing, though, how quickly patients become accustomed to our routine. Their first natural sensations of homesickness lessen as soon as the feeling of returning strength appears. Sad thoughts vanish like snow before the sun. Of course, there may come times to all of them when I see depression, but this is usually due to out-side causes—bad news from home—not because of association with others who are ill, some perhaps more ill than themselves."

The two men spent several hours going over the sanatorium records, discussing problems of administration and of fund-raising. As they were exchanging views of recent articles, the door opened and a nurse said, "Could you come out for a minute, Dr. Trudeau? Miss Henle in Little Red has begun to hemorrhage."

When Trudeau entered the cottage a few minutes later, he looked into the frightened eyes of a young girl and saw the kidney-shaped pan at her chin, half full of blood. Her roommate was quite calm, putting cold packs on the girl's chest and trying to comfort her.

"The bleeding has about stopped, I think," the girl said as she replaced the wet cloth.

"You did fine. Thanks," he said as he sat on the chair by the bed and took the sick patient's hand. "You bled far less this time, Miss Henle. It might even have done you some good, brought up a few bugs from your lung. Now, don't worry. I'll be around for a while. The nurse will stay with you."

The bleeding was over. As Trudeau re-entered the office, he said to Bowditch, "A sad case. Been here only two weeks. She is not seriously ill. Fear is her worst enemy. I'm sorry she has no religion. It would be a great help."

Dr. Bowditch and the nurse exchanged glances. The nurse spoke: "I'll go out there. I'm so glad you were here, Dr. Trudeau. She'll calm down now. You can even make dying seem like a great adventure. I've seen you do that."

"I guess it takes more than buildings and money to make a good sanatorium," Dr. Bowditch said as they left for town.

Trudeau seldom had a more willing listener, a more enthusiastic physician to talk with about his work. It was a joy to have Dr. Bowditch as his guest. The visit provided a welcome diversion for Lottie too. When night came and Francis was in bed, Chatte quiet with the light out and ready to sleep, she brought her mending into the parlor and sat in front of the fire, listening to the men "talk shop." Ned, pretending to study, was there too. When Dr. Bowditch himself pleaded weariness they all said good night. For the first time in months Trudeau slept well, but as soon as his visitor had departed he returned to his evening laboratory work.

If the direct annihilation of the bacillus by germicides was hopeless, would it be possible to find a substance derived from cultures of bacillus which would help? This question was a natural consequence of Koch's discovery of the tubercle bacillus and Pasteur's work on anthrax, chicken cholera and hydrophobia. If inoculations prevented these diseases, why couldn't they do the same for tuberculosis? If this were possible, the road lay open for a cure. He would try to produce immunity in his animals with dead germs first, then try inoculations derived from liquid cultures of filtered living bacilli.

Once again Ned supplied the pen with rabbits. Once again his father began the long, tedious work. Trudeau had no illusions. He felt that there was precious little in the clinical history of tuberculosis to foster much hope that any method of protective inoculation was likely to work in this disease, but he must try. After two series of inoculations performed in the spring and summer of 1890, one with nonliving chemical products of the bacillus, the other with attenuated but living cultures, he admitted that his fears were well founded. With a weary heart he sat down to write his article.

"Why is it," he asked himself, "that some who are poorly fed and housed get tuberculosis and others in a like situation do not?" This was the question. His inoculations with cultures from a living bacilli did seem to offer a brief, small degree of immunity in animals, but only in isolated cases. There must be something in natural immunity. Take Chatte, for instance. She had always received the best of food and care, had lived in the open and developed a strong, muscular body; yet only a few short months in New York brought her this deadly illnes. Others, who all their lives were exposed to bad living conditions, managed to escape. Mere physical vigor might be a prominent element in some cases, environment too—but they were not the whole story.

Impatiently Trudeau threw his pencil aside and left the laboratory. The more he tried to think his conclusions through, the more confused he became. His mind was getting fuzzy. He must get away from these problems for a few weeks.

On the evening of August 7, 1890, he opened the New York *Times*, which had arrived on the morning train. On the front page was a report of meetings of the International Congress of Physicians, in Berlin. Professor Rudolf Virchow, a pathologist who was the first to define scrofula as a distinct disease of the lympathic glands, was president this year. Following a summary of his address, the report listed other speakers, including Professor Robert Koch who read a paper, "Bacteriology," in which he referred to the good results of the discovery of the tubercle bacillus.

Trudeau grunted.

Lottie, who had just entered the room after giving Chatte a glass of milk, asked, "I'm glad to see you take an evening off, dear, but what are you reading that disgusts you so much?"

Trudeau tossed the paper onto his footstool. "Oh, just about Koch. He is as usual reminding the assemblage of his great discovery. As if any of us would be likely to forget. I had hoped that he'd say something new."

The next few weeks were busy one, mostly filled with sanatorium problems, fund-raising, new additions to the administration building that were long overdue, the demand for higher wages, more beds, the problems of unskilled help. Good as several of the practical nurses were, he wished that he could afford well-trained ones such as they now had at Bellevue and other large hospitals. Unfortunately he could not afford to hire people like that, even if he could persuade them to come to Saranac. He was finally forced to hire a new superintendent, since the job of supervising the plant and nursing was too much for the Nortons. Mrs. Julia Miller was a boon to the weary physician, for she proved faithful and capable and had previous experience as manager of a boardinghouse in Saranac Lake. Even she could not be expected to work miracles with unskilled help.

The report on the Berlin Congress appeared in the September issues of the medical journals. To Trudeau's astonishment he discovered that Koch, far from merely parading his past achievements before the Congress, had announced his discovery of a substance which "would completely immunize guinea-pigs against subsequent inoculations with the tubercle bacilli, and would *cure* the disease in human beings."

A cure!

It was past midnight when Trudeau found this announcement. He had a raging headache, and his eyes were bloodshot from steady reading by lamplight, so at first he thought that he might have mis-read the report. No, there was the simple statement in cold type—Koch had found the answer!

It was incredible. As he had so many years earlier when he read about Koch's discovery of the bacillus, Trudeau frantically leafed through the other journals on the table. Again, there was only one brief statement—no details, no key as to the actual method. Ex-hausted though he was, Trudeau wrote to Walton and Loomis, begging them to comment on Koch's report.

"Naturally, I am much excited about this development," Dr. Loomis replied. "The men who returned from the Congress say Koch claims his vaccine is dangerous to prepare, so for the time-being he will not reveal details. I am sure he will have to soon, if only to protect his reputation."

According to an article in the *Times*, headed, "The Secret of the Lymph," Koch called his preparation, "tuberculin," and said that in his opinion it was best to allow the experiments to proceed in Berlin, performed by physicians who would not be swayed by knowl-edge of its content. He insisted that he knew it was successful. The reporter had interviewed Loomis who said, "This explanation is incomplete and unsatisfactory."

Dr. Janeway was quoted as saying, "I will reserve judgment until I am able to test the substance in my own laboratory."

Apparently it did not occur to any journalist to interview Edward Livingston Trudeau. It is doubtful that they even knew his name at this time, but the lone physician and scientist in the north woods was not disturbed by this slight. He was too engrossed in wondering about the exact formula to think of publicity. He was delighted when he received a letter from Dr. Osler in Baltimore, saying that the Koch laboratory had promised to send him samples of tuberculin and that he would forward a vial to Saranac Lake.

Trudeau's patient, George Cooper, had read the reports in the newspapers and was very excited. "I will pay the cost of your passage to Berlin. Find out firsthand about this vaccine."

Trudeau hesitated, then wrote to Dr. Prudden, asking his advice: should he go to Berlin?

Dr. Prudden said, "No. The Germans are cagey. I doubt that you would get inside the gates. Koch seems to want his country to get all the credit and a monopoly on manufacture."

In spite of Trudeau's attempts to keep everyone calm, he was helpless. The patients, who had read the sensational stories about the new "cure," could talk of little else. "How soon will you get this serum? Does it make you well with the first shot?"

He had but one answer: "Do not let your hopes get too high. We must keep calm until we know more."

He might as well have told the Saranac River to change its course. The little city of the sick became a city with just one thought. Certain that the tedious rest cure would soon go into discard, several bed patients violated the sanatorium rules by walking into town. Others, some very sick ones, talked of getting someone to pay their passage to Bremen. One night two patients packed their belongings and announced that they were going to New York to ask Dr. Loomis to give them shots of the "miracle vaccine."

In an attempt to restore order, Trudeau explained that neither Loomis nor any other New Yorker had samples of tuberculin, that Osler would be the first to receive them, that he promised to send some to Saranac. Excitement increased.

Meanwhile Trudeau repeated his experiments with the bacilli, using guinea pigs and rabbits, but with the same negative results. He wondered whether he should bother to write up his own report, but since Koch had not revealed his secret, and apparently would not do so for many months, he might as well. They were of historical interest, if nothing else. He felt that his observations on immunity might have some permanent value.

Following the first paragraph he had begun earlier, he wrote:

The margin between susceptibility and immunity, biological or chemical, is very narrow. The most promise lies in the study of natures laws of immunity and how to imitate them . . . Immunity may be due to the germicidal power of the blood serum, some think, or to cell activity, or to the susceptibility of nerve centers to attack by microbes.

In conclusion he referred to Koch:

Merely as a biological study of the tubercle bacillus these observations seem perhaps worthy of record, and we may, in spite of unpromising evidence, turn to the brilliant announcements recently published with a strong hope that the resources of foreign laboratories or the individual efforts of some earnest workers are about to solve the problem of protective inoculation for this disease, even if the genius of Koch, reaching out along new lines, has not already succeeded in producing a specific treatment for the cure of tuberculosis.

This article, which appeared in a November, 1890, issue of the *Medical Record*, was, in the opinion of twentieth-century specialists, one of the most important contributions in the field to come from any American scientist, but few of Trudeau's contemporaries realized this. They may have been too preoccupied with Koch's puzzling announcement. Actually, it was ten years later, when Paul Roemer in Germany followed the same thinking and issued identical conclusions, that the nature of immunity in tuberculosis received marked attention. Men had forgotten. Trudeau did not receive the credit. Even Dr. Osler was still clinging to the theory that inheritance was the single important factor in the development of tuberculosis.

When the first small bulb of tuberculin finally arrived, patients who had been unwilling to try earlier cures begged to be the first to receive the new serum. Trudeau selected only those with the best chances for recovery. He began with very small injections and made daily trips to see each patient, watching for results. A week passed, then a month, two months—there was no sign of change. Gradually he began to worry and spoke to Lottie about it. "Surely, a man like Koch would not foist a worthless drug on the world!"

At last, in January, in response to world-wide pressure, Dr. Koch revealed his secret. The magic fluid for which people had offered as much as one thousand dollars an ounce, which inspired crowds to parade in the streets of Berlin chanting the name of Robert Koch, was nothing more than live filtered cultures of tubercle bacilli in glycerin!

Trudeau had a dozen vials in his own laboratory, duplicates of the substances he used in his futile attempts to immunize rabbits and guinea pigs—exactly like the material Koch had discovered.

As one experimenter after another tried tuberculin with the same negative results, the medical world began to scoff. The great scientist, the discoverer of the tubercle bacillus, the idol of the world of bacteriology, was now hailed as a fraud!

Trudeau did not join in the denunciation. Was there something unusual in the way the German used tuberculin? Why should a man who was so careful in describing his early work not give details of his present work? Without them no one could duplicate, confirm or deny the results.

The next few months and years brought no adequate explanation. Koch never clearly explained his reasons for making this hasty and premature claim for tuberculin, and it remains one of the medical world's great mysteries.

XVI.

DISTRACTIONS

▣▣▣

Trudeau always kept detailed records of his laboratory work, and while he knew that he should do the same for all his patients, he lacked time, energy and inclination. His memory was far above the average, so that he knew the details of every patient's illness. Unfortunately, this would be of little help when a much-needed resident physician came to share the burden at the sanatorium. Up to now Trudeau did not have the money for this luxury, so he carried on as best he could.

For years Charles Lea had urged him to start an endowment fund for the institution, but it was not until Loomis made veiled remarks which led Trudeau to believe that the sanatorium might go bankrupt that he turned his attention to this important problem. Once again Ed Harriman came to the rescue and secured a banker who was willing to help raise the money in New York. While Mr. Stephen Baker agreed to the task reluctantly, and said that he would have to turn it over to someone else when he reached the goal of fifty thousand dollars, he was still on the job when the endowment boasted ten times that amount twenty years later.

Many of Trudeau's early friends were gone now. Julia Livingston had died, and so had Jim. Lou was in ill health and spending much of his time in Rome. The Livingston brothers had never shown much interest in Trudeau's sanatorium, but he missed chances to chat with them in New York. While the summer residents continued their support, the burden of making up an annual deficit of twelve thousand dollars was a great strain.

Now that Saranac had gained considerable renown, a few new donors joined the old. Trudeau's correspondence assumed heavy proportions, and while most of it was friendly, there were frequent critical letters too. One day a patient showed Trudeau a letter from a businessman in his home town. "What sort of a man is Trudeau?" the writer asked. "Is he what so many say he is or just a clever doctor who has made a fortune out of the Adirondacks?"

Trudeau exploded. "If giving patients care at half-price, if running up a big deficit is making a man rich, then I have a good thing here. I am always puzzled to know why people cannot understand the spirit of this work. I draw no salary. I don't own a cent of the sanatorium money!"

This letter still rankled him weeks later when a well-meaning friend surprised him with a fine new carriage and young horse to replace Kitty. "I can't ride in that thing," he protested. "People will think I don't need money for my sanatorium!"

When his friend pointed out the bad condition of his own carriage and remarked that Kitty was getting lame, he relented.

Saranac Lake village was bursting at the seams by 1891. From a dozen scattered homes, the place now spread along the slope above the river, and had almost five thousand inhabitants. Trudeau realized that he could no longer handle all the practice. He had to have an assistant. Good friends would provide the money.

Dr. Irwin Hance, a slightly built man just out of medical school, agreed to come as the first resident physician at a salary of sixty dollars a month. It was a wonderful relief to have him there for two years, ready for emergencies that up to now had always called Trudeau to the mountaintop.

But Dr. Hance also was drawn into experiments. Trudeau had heard that people said Saranac was full of germs, that it was not safe for healthy folks to go there. This was most upsetting, since great stress had always been placed on hygiene, the patients trained to spit into disposable gauze, to cover their mouths when they coughed, and to be most careful about washing their hands. He had even set up a sanitary code for the village—and it became the model for New York City. Since the rumors continued, Dr. Hance agreed to play a part in stopping them.

"I want you to collect dust from the walls of all the buildings and then inject a sample from each building into separate lots of guinea pigs," Trudeau explained. "We will do the same in town."

A few weeks later the inoculated guinea pigs were still hopping around in their pens, free from any signs of tuberculosis.

A logical outcome of this research was a growing awareness on the part of some physicians of the need for governmental action. Under the leadership of Dr. Herman Biggs, New York City established in 1892 the first Health Department diagnostic laboratory and eventually succeeded in having tuberculous patients segregated in the city's hospitals. Campaigns, for several years unsuccessful, tried to force legislation requiring registration of all known tuberculous patients. But this smacked of interference in the relationship between physi-

cian and patient, and powerful medical men fought it every foot of
the way, in spite of Trudeau's contention that it was vital to general
public health.

He insisted that doctors needed special training in order to
diagnose tuberculosis in its earliest stages. Again, certain powerful
societies scoffed. And he watched with bitter feelings as young Dr.
Lawrence Flick in Philadelphia tried to get physicians to join the
public in a society for the prevention of the spread of the disease.
Dr. Bowditch did get his sanatorium though, and plans were being
made by the state of Massachusetts to build a publicly supported
institution. A scattered few other hospitals devoted exclusively to
treatment of the tuberculous were being planned. In spite of these
encouraging signs, the over-all problem looked monumental.

One of the most vexing was the power of medical "cults." By far
the largest was that of the homeopaths, who followed the theories
held by Dr. Samuel Hahnemann of Leipzig. Hahnemann in 1800
said that a drug that will produce certain disease *symptoms* in a
healthy person will cure a sick one of that disease. Dr. Oliver Wen-
dell Holmes of Boston was the first American physician to attack
homeopathy with vigor, in an article, "Homeopathy and Its Kindred
Delusions," printed in 1841. In his characteristic manner, Holmes
poked fun at these practitioners, asking why, if like cures like,
arsenic could not cure the mischief which arsenic causes, and
why smallpox did not remedy the disease it produced. He hastened
to add that the virus used in vaccination does not cure smallpox,
but rather prevents it by inducing a slight case—the only known
prevention at that time. He ridiculed the infinitesimal doses of medicine used by the homeopaths as entirely ineffective, and set down
an array of mathematical calculations to drive home his point.

Trudeau, like nearly all medical men, was well acquainted with
this masterpiece of logical medical prose. His theories, like that of
all "regular" physicians, whom the homeopaths referred to as allo-
paths, ran directly counter to theirs. He believed in using drugs to
counteract symptoms. But homeopathy had a strong foothold in the
United States, and some of the most prominent laymen in the
country depended on doctors who were homeopaths.

In the summer of 1892 the papers were full of reports about Mrs. Benjamin Harrison, the wife of the president, who suffered from tuberculosis. Her family physician was a homeopath named Gardner. When in September he told the press that Mrs. Harrison was going to the north woods for a rest, Trudeau was startled. It seemed to him a risky move for so sick a patient. He was pleased that the President visited Saranac Lake while he and his wife were guests of the Whitelaw Reids, but he was embarrassed when the President asked that he be called in on "consultation."

Trudeau knew that Dr. Gardner must look on this move with sad misgivings, and went to the Reid's house, expecting a cold reception from the homeopathic physician. As he entered, President Harrison met him and said, "She has taken a turn for the worse. A complication."

Trudeau found that Dr. Gardner had called in a nerve specialist, a Dr. Dougherty from New York. When they led him to the sickroom, he saw that Mrs. Harrison was indeed very ill and especially short of breath. He did not have to use a thermometer to know that she had a very high fever. The minute he began his examination he told the doctors that there was a large amount of fluid in her chest cavity. "We must draw this off. That will lower the fever and allow her to breathe more easily."

The two men shook their heads in unison.

Seeing this, Trudeau folded his stethoscope and arose. "Think it over. It's not a dangerous procedure. If you want me to do it, I'll come back tomorrow." He knew that Gardner would never be convinced that even this simple surgical technique could be of help to Mrs. Harrison. It would conflict with his theory that "like cures like."

The next day Trudeau was called to the Reids' home. When he again entered the sickroom, Dr. Gardner and Dr. Dougherty were literally wringing their hands. Without a word Trudeau took out his trocar and tapped off some fluid from the patient's right side.

Immediately she announced that she felt better.

Feeling it unwise to draw off all the fluid in one operation, he promised to return the next day and complete the task, giving Mrs.

Harrison time to gain a little strength in the meantime. As he spoke, Trudeau sized up the expressions on the faces of the doctors. They were identical—a mixture of fear and chagrin. In order to avoid a misconception Trudeau felt that he must be perfectly frank. When they all met with the President, he said, "I see no hope for recovery. The disease is too extensive, and her general condition is poor."

Dr. Dougherty bristled. "I do not agree! Mrs. Harrison's real trouble is weak nerves. She needs to get back to the White House where she can be free of these distractions."

Trudeau had difficulty in restraining his impatience. "I see no reason why she should not return if she feels strong enough."

Again he watched the papers, to see just what the Harrison physicians would say for the benefit of the curious public. Two days later the *Times* reported:

> The operations were performed under the most alarming conditions and were resorted to only as extreme measures. On both occasions the patient's system sustained the operations with difficulty. There was immediate danger of fatality. One of the doctors said today that he would not have been surprised if she died during it.

The following report was that Mrs. Harrison was much better, and a few days later she returned to the White House. She died on the morning of October 25.

There followed a flurry of articles, an exchange of accusations by doctors representing the two schools. Trudeau's temper boiled when a leading medical journal printed the accusation that his treatment had shortened the woman's life. He canceled his subscription.

One December morning, when Ned was home for vacation from his first year at Yale and Chatte was so ill that Trudeau despaired of her life, he was up early, unable to sleep. The doorbell rang. Curious to know who could be calling at this hour—six o'clock— he rushed to the door. He was surprised to see a slender, dark-haired young man standing there, a gentle smile on his face.

"I saw you walking around," he said in a quiet voice. "I am

Edward R. Baldwin from New Haven. You are Dr. Trudeau, of course?"

"Sit down while I stir up the fire. What brings you all the way from New Haven on the night train?"

"I'm a physician, just out of Yale. I have tuberculosis."

Trudeau put down the poker. "What gives you that idea?"

"I found the bacilli in my sputum under my microscope."

Trudeau did not know whether to congratulate Dr. Baldwin or to sympathize with him. The gospel of scientific tests had indeed spread when a young physician actually looked at his own sputum!

The arrival of Baldwin opened a new era in Saranac Lake. For the first time Trudeau acquired a patient who shared his enthusiasm for the laboratory. The young doctor had to wait six weeks before a bed became vacant at the Adirondack Cottage Sanitarium, and while he was living at the hotel, he formed the habit of dropping in at the laboratory. Trudeau was happy to show him all he knew about experiments, and by the time Dr. Baldwin began his official cure, Trudeau knew that he had acquired a partner, a dedicated physician-scientist who intended to remain in Saranac, to devote his life to the care of the tuberculous, to the search for a cure. Baldwin would draw bare living expenses in the way of salary, but this was enough for him during these early years.

Through good luck as much as good sense, Trudeau had managed to keep his illness in check through the years, but these later strains and hard work as well as worry, were taking their toll. It was a great comfort to have the quiet, understanding colleague to share his burden. Every evening, while Francis played at their feet, the two men could be seen at the window, reading and talking. Trudeau translated the French medical journals, while Baldwin translated those printed in German.

Sometimes these regular sessions were interrupted by visitors— Ed Harriman, Dr. Osler, Dr. Welch, Dr. Bowditch, Charles Lea and, on one occasion, by William Howard Taft. These evenings were stimulating to Trudeau, who acted as a kind of moderator on all subjects, drawing the best from each speaker, his eyes sparkling with enthusiasm. But nearly always the conversation finally returned to the subject close to his heart, and the great laymen who happened to be present found that Trudeau was a master at making his own "shop talk" understandable and interesting. As for himself, he looked on these gatherings as a sign that he was no longer a lonely searcher carrying a single lamp in the northern wilderness.

But the lamp in the small bedroom off the parlor finally went out. Chatte died on March 30, 1893. Again old friends came from New York, in a long train furnished by Harriman. Paul Smith and his sons covered the snow around St. John's in the Wilderness with evergreen boughs just before the service. It was simple and beautiful, this service, as Chatte had wanted it to be. Her brother Ned, the Smith boys, her old playmates served as pallbearers.

All the way home through the darkness Trudeau thought of the four long years during which Chatte fought for her life while he went on with his search for a cure. She was gone, but his determination was as great as ever—perhaps, he felt, even greater.

XVII.

OUT OF THE ASHES

◻◻◻

Chatte's death left Trudeau exhausted and ill. He lost more weight, suffered from frequent headaches and caught every illness that he was exposed to, or so it appeared. Francis came down with whooping cough; so did he, and when he recovered from that, he had a bad attack of influenza. Fortunately, in spite of her own grief, Lottie remained well throughout this ordeal, always ready to help lift her husband's dragging spirits. Ned, and doing very well at Yale, was a comfort to offset their sorrow.

In spite of all his troubles Trudeau continued his interest in scientific experiments and produced a number of significant articles, one of them on the contagiousness of influenza. He also made studies on variations in growth of the tubercle bacilli and increased his experiments with tuberculin, trying each modification of Koch's discovery as it was announced in the medical journals. Nothing much came of them except reinforcement of his theory that only a limited amount of immunity to tuberculosis could be obtained, and that through prior infection from the bacillus.

Late in the summer of 1893 he again fell ill with a distressing kidney complaint that kept him out of his beloved laboratory for several months. He had to give up his regular monthly examination of patients at the sanatorium and curtail his practice in town. By November he felt well enough to go to New York with Lottie on his annual fund-raising expedition.

Luis Walton rushed over to the hotel and after one look at his friend sent for Dr. Loomis. As it happened, Loomis himself was not too well at this time. He called in other physicians, and after many tests and much consultation, they announced that it was an abscessed kidney.

"Wouldn't you know," Trudeau asked, "after all these years of fighting the tiger that something like this would jump on me?" He was disgusted, for he had several good prospects for large contributions and could not do much about them from his bed in the hotel.

Gradually the pain subsided enough to allow him to sleep. He had been ill for about a week when the trained nurse whom Loomis had sent to care for him came to the door at nine o'clock in the morning with the news that someone was in the hotel parlor. "He wants to talk with you, Mrs. Trudeau."

"Who is it?" Trudeau asked, fearing the worst.

After what seemed a long time but was actually only fifteen minutes, Lottie returned. He could see from the expression on her face that she did have bad news.

She sat in the chair by his bed and grasped his thin fingers in hers. "I have always told you everything, and I see no reason to hide news from you now, sick as you are, my dear." Her voice was calm and low.

Immediately the thought flashed through Trudeau's mind that Ned was desperately ill or even dead. He lay there trembling.

Then the nurse opened the door, and in walked Dr. Loomis, looking very solemn.

"Well, tell me, somebody. What is it? Is it Ned?"

"Oh dear me, no!" Lottie said quickly. She turned to Loomis. "You tell him, doctor."

"Dr. Baldwin has just wired me that your house was destroyed by fire. No one was hurt. Francis was at his home, as you know." Loomis stood behind Lottie's chair, now, speaking rapidly. "The fire started from the little incubator lamp in the laboratory. Almost nothing was saved."

Trudeau, who had half risen and was leaning on one hand, dropped back to the pillow. "Oh, is that all? Why on earth didn't you say so right away? We can get another house."

Dr. Loomis looked first at him, then in astonishment at Lottie. "Well, I must get to the office," he said as he picked up his wraps and hurried from the room.

Trudeau's next concern was for Dr. Baldwin. "Lottie, get a pencil. I must send him a telegram at once. He'll worry for fear I think he was to blame. It must have been a great shock to the poor fellow. Now, tell him not to worry about the loss of the house and laboratory. As soon as I get well we will build again."

He was surprised when he saw what wide newspaper publicity the fire received. Telegrams and letters poured into the hotel; one of them from Dr. Osler which read: *Dear Trudeau, there is nothing like a fire to make a man do the Phoenix trick.*

When he read this from his good friend in Baltimore, Trudeau realized for the first time that his assurance to Baldwin had been on the optimistic side. He would do well, indeed, to raise his laboratory out of the ashes! But where would he find the money to replace all that equipment? And what about his records? If he could get back on his feet, be rid of the gnawing pain in his back, he would no doubt look on this as a challenge. At the moment the loss at Saranac seemed irreplaceable.

To add to his woes, the insurance people argued that his policy did not cover loss due to an unattended laboratory lamp, but finally, after much haggling, they agreed to pay the full amount covering the house, provided he would sign a paper admitting that the fire was due to negligence. At least he could rebuild their home.

One evening, when Lottie sat by the bed reading to him, trying to take his mind off his troubles, in walked Dr. Eugene Hodenpyl, carrying a large box. He smiled as he crossed the room. "I know I should not have come in at this hour, and there's no real excuse except—well—the boys at the laboratory heard about your fire. Dr. Baldwin wrote that your microscope was lost, so the boys chipped in to get you a new one."

Trudeau was so overcome by this generosity that he stammered, "Oh, I, well, how nice!"

Before he could say another word, his friend had bowed himself out of the room. Trudeau was still so surprised that it did not occur to him to send Lottie after the retreating Hodenpyl so that he could thank him properly. What a beautiful instrument it was! Much finer than his old one, just as up-to-date as Dr. Prudden's. He *must* get money to build a laboratory now.

He was in no condition to plan for anything during the next few months. It was late spring before they returned to Saranac, staying first in Mr. Cooper's cottage, then later in the St. Luke rectory, while Larry Aspinwall's plans for a new home materialized.

Trudeau still had no plans for a laboratory, expecting once again to build a simple workroom, this time unattached to the house.

When Mr. Cooper asked him about it, Trudeau said that he hoped to find a few thousand dollars somewhere, but he had not looked into the matter seriously.

Cooper smiled. "It's time for you to think about it seriously, doctor. I have. Now, my plan is to give you enough to build as fine a laboratory as you need—complete with self-regulating thermo-stats, gas, electricity and, in fact, every convenience to make your work easy."

Did any man ever have such good friends? Cooper and his sister, who had already done so much for the sanatorium, were now making an even greater offer of help. "How can I thank you? How can I?"

"Well, we'll name the laboratory for you, doctor. That is the way you can thank me. You won't let us call the sanatorium by your name. At least the laboratory should . . ."

Trudeau was indignant. "The idea! Why should it have my name? It is to be the George C. Cooper Laboratory for the Study of Tuberculosis!"

Cooper frowned. "I withdraw my offer!"

For a moment Trudeau thought the man was joking, but he could see now from the stern look in his eyes that he was not. Reluctantly, in a weak voice of defeat, he said, "Well, I cannot afford to lose your generous offer. Suppose we call it the Saranac Laboratory for the Study of Tuberculosis?"

Cooper laughed and shook his head, perplexed. "Why are you so stubborn?"

"Why are you?" Trudeau asked.

"Well, all right. We will name it for the town."

While the square, stone, two-story building on Church Street, directly behind the new house, was under construction, Trudeau drew up a set of rules that would always govern the policies and practices of the laboratory. It was to be devoted to pure research. Any results obtained from experiments would be furnished willingly and free of charge for the use of other scientists. No one would ever be able to accuse this laboratory of selfishness. It would devote its efforts to the good of all mankind and not hoard its secrets for the benefit and profit of one organization or one country. Its failures and successes were open to all investigators. Thus opened in 1894 the first complete laboratory in the United States, devoted exclusively to the study of tuberculosis—a fine, beautifully equipped successor to that small lean-to that had housed Trudeau's first historic experiments.

One of the most vexing problems that occupied Trudeau during his convalescence from his kidney trouble was that of recurrence of tuberculosis in those who left the sanatorium apparently cured. Almost three-fourths of these people again fell ill, often after returning to their homes and jobs. He realized that while the former patients might do their best to live simple, well-regulated lives, their families, friends and employers often saw no reason for caution, thinking that since they looked well, they had nothing further to worry about.

A way had to be found to meet this danger, to educate the general public and the profession, to stress the need for follow-up medical care and prompt action in order to protect the ill and save others from infection. What could he or his assistants do from Saranac? Dr. Herman Biggs, Dr. Lawrence Flick, Dr. William Osler, Dr. Loomis and other physicians in various parts of the country were making a strenuous effort, but the campaign needed funds and centralized direction. While Trudeau was thinking about this problem and what to say to Dr. Loomis when he next saw him, news came that his good friend and colleague had died.

The strong arm of the Adirondack Cottage Sanitarium in New York, his chief dependence through these early years, was gone. And it came at a time when Loomis was planning to open his own sanitarium in Sullivan County, where he could try out his own ideas, experiment with the important problem of graded work exercises during convalescence. His death was a personal loss to Trudeau and to the country.

The telegram said that the physician had died from a hemorrhage. "How strange," he remarked to Lottie, "the Lord allows me and my old frame to carry on and takes away so unexpectedly a man like Loomis who thought he had his tiger licked." Loomis had not looked well; as Trudeau thought back to his visit in New York, he remembered this.

Trudeau never knew just how much tuberculosis Loomis had. Certainly he had appeared to lead a normal life. But so it went. He must have had those bacilli lurking, waiting somewhere in the hidden recesses of his lungs. A severe case of influenza was all the old TB bugs needed to strike him down.

Dr. Walter B. James, a noted New York physician, agreed to take over Loomis' work for the Adirondack Cottage Sanitarium, and while Trudeau knew that he was lucky to have him, it was many weeks before he stopped fretting about the death of Dr. Loomis.

During this period he found it more and more difficult to bear his troubles, and visitors were often at a loss to know how to deal with him. If they remarked that he had gained weight and looked fine, the corners of his mouth would go down and he would launch into a chronicle of his complaints. If they said something sympathetic, he looked unhappy and talked about Loomis and how you never knew when you would die. Wise visitors soon learned that if they forgot personal remarks and concentrated on talk about experiments in the laboratory or new buildings at the sanatorium, Trudeau radiated optimism.

There was so much to do, so little time left, yet the thought of his laboratory, his unfinished experiments, sparked new life.

Trudeau often marveled at how much of his life's activities developed by mere chance. "If Frank had not died, would I have studied medicine? If the Livingstons had not brought me up to St. Regis, would I have lived to work at all? If Lottie had not been willing to come to these back woods, would I have started my sanatorium?"

Another chance event reorganized his life. It happened one warm August day in 1898, on a ride from St. Regis to Saranac Lake. As he looked back on it now, five years later, he saw that it was one of those milestones, as important as the chance appearance of Dr. Baldwin. Lawrason Brown, a young medical student from Johns Hopkins, had contracted tuberculosis and was teaching school at St. Regis, recuperating in the bracing mountain air. One day he asked Trudeau if he might visit the sanatorium.

Brown was a charming, soft-voiced, vivacious young man with a fine mind, and, according to Dr. Osler, a "born physician."

Eager to make the young man feel completely at ease, Trudeau talked frankly about his work and problems, asking Brown for suggestions, particularly in getting patients back on their feet and ensuring, as far as possible, a permanent arrest of their disease.

Rather shyly Brown said, "Well, doctor, I have had only three years in medical school, but I do know that convalescence is a dangerous period for the patient, even though his lesions appear healed."

Eager to draw the young man out, Trudeau put his question

another way: "You have personal experience in this problem. If you had the responsibility for cases, what would you do?"

Brown thought a while as the horse turned down the hill above Saranac Lake, then he said, "Well, I'd give them gradual exercise, ask them to help make beds, empty baskets, serve meals, perhaps, just as I've heard you are doing now."

Trudeau brightened. This fellow had more than a casual interest. He waited for him to continue.

"I've thought that it's important to keep one's mind and hands occupied with easy, useful tasks."

As they rode through the town and up toward the sanatorium, Brown asked whether it might be possible to start a handcraft shop for patients able to be up a large part of the day.

"That's an excellent idea! Ah, we must do that, we must—only, who is to start it? I don't have time nor talent along that line."

Three years later, after Brown had regained his health and finished his medical schooling, he returned to Saranac Lake to become assistant to the new resident physician at the sanatorium, Dr. C. C. Trembley. Once again this was no short-term affair, a mere basis for later practice in distant cities. Dr. Lawrason Brown was here to stay. He set up a careful record system for all patients; he opened a tent-covered hobby shop; he developed graded exercise and work schedules along careful lines; he enlarged the sanatorium library; he started a small publication, *The Journal of Outdoor Life,* a magazine for patients which later developed a national circulation.

Trudeau, at fifty-five, was the leading practitioner in his field of medicine, known both in Europe and the United States as the guiding spirit in the fight against tuberculosis; and as such he came in for a long string of honors. Columbia University was the first institution to honor him, officially, with the degree of Master of Science and membership on the Board of Trustees of the medical college. Trudeau was not able to attend the ceremony, but he was pleased as well as amused. Here he was, one of the least promising graduates of the college, raised to this exalted state!

The same could not be said for his son Ned. From the day he

entered the College of Physicians and Surgeons he had been at the head of his class, recognized as one of the most promising students in recent years. While the boy was never as husky in appearance as Chatte and Francis, he was wiry, with good resistance to infections. He had been captain of the Yale baseball team, and later president of his class when he graduated from medical school in 1900. After a year as intern at Presbyterian Hospital in New York, he announced that he wanted to set up practice for himself.

Trudeau knew that he had received two offers of partnership and naturally expected him to accept one of them.

"No, Father, I would rather settle here," he said.

Tears came into Trudeau's eyes when he heard this. It would be wonderful to have Ned here, but he must not stand in the way of a brilliant career. "Son, you know as well as I that this would be a poor choice. You have never had TB. Now Brown and Baldwin have, so it's easy to see why they stay in these woods. But you should not—it would limit your chances for advancement. Take the offer from Dr. Walter James. Go to New York."

After a few days Ned agreed. He went to New York. Trudeau and Lottie read each letter about his work with pleasure and pride. Dr. James sent glowing reports throughout the winter of 1903-04, and they looked forward to seeing their son in his own office as assistant to this fine physician. Then in spring James sent a telegram:

Ned has come down with an acute pneumonia. I urge you to come by the earliest train. Stay at my house.

Trudeau would often claim that he did not sleep a wink all night. This time it was true. As he and Lottie boarded the night sleeper for New York, neither had much to say. They tossed in their berths, looked out into the darkness, watched the flickering lights in lonely farmhouses and waited for dawn.

Dr. James met them at the train and took them immediately to Presbyterian Hospital. Trudeau saw that his son was dangerously ill. He and Lottie spent five long, anxious days, then at last Dr. James announced, "The fever is down. I've just come from the hospital. The crisis is passed. I think you can take him home in about ten days."

All that morning the Trudeaus counted their fortunes, prayed and received congratulations from friends who, like themselves, had waited with fear and trembling. That afternoon toward sundown Ned had a heart attack and died.

Once again Larry Aspinwall, Luis Walton—all their good city friends—gathered around to help soften the blow. Harriman, with his customary generosity, provided special cars to carry Ned, his friends, the flowers and sorrowing friends back to the Adirondacks. Paul Smith waited at the northern end of the line, his hotel open to receive all the guests. The entire community turned out to help in any way they could. The livery-stable men had their horses curried, their hacks polished ready for the services at the little church in the wilderness. When it was all over, Trudeau asked Paul Smith what he owed him.

"Out of my way! Can't you understand how my missus and I and my boys feel?"

It was the same with the livery-stable men and their drivers, the same at the florist's shop and at the undertaker's. No one would take any money.

Old Fitz Halleck finally explained, "You see, doctor, we all loved that boy. You mustn't insult us with money. Love you can't buy. What would this town be without you? We'd all starve to death or live on rabbit meat, I reckon."

XVIII.

THE OPTIMIST

The next few years were the most difficult in Trudeau's life. Even Lottie staggered under this new blow, but gradually they both managed to overcome the sharp reality of their grief.

It was fortunate that Trudeau was able to keep himself occupied with plans for the future of his sanatorium. By 1910 there were thirty-one buildings and twenty-four cottages on Mount Pisgah. Three resident physicians and five trained nurses supervised the care of the 110 patients, many of whom were permitted to stay out of bed nearly all day, except for two hours of rest in the afternoon. The hobby-shop program was growing so rapidly and had proven so successful that it had to have permanent quarters. There was a new administration building, an infirmary-hospital for bedridden patients, a medical building where tests, examinations and laboratory work were taken care of, and various service structures necessary to provide laundry, heat and general maintenance. Never at any period had Trudeau visualized a really large sanatorium. His idea remained that of developing a model institution for the care of the tuberculous who had more than "a fighting chance" for recovery when they were admitted. Also, he refused to consider admitting people who could afford to go elsewhere.

An important aid—the most important since Trudeau hired his first resident physician—was the X ray, a penetrating ray by means of which the entire chest, as well as other body parts could be photographed, allowing scientists and physicians to see through the flesh and opaque objects. This important development in diagnosis was the discovery of a German scientist, Wilhelm Konrad Roentgen of Würzberg, in 1895, but the X-ray machine was expensive and at that time dangerous to use. It was 1913 before Trudeau was able to install one at the Adirondack Cottage Sanitarium, with a trained operator to supervise its use.

Another important development came at about the same time: artificial pneumothorax, a method of introducing gas or air into the pleural cavity by needle, causing the lung or a part of it to collapse temporarily, thus allowing the organ to rest and therefore heal more rapidly. Trudeau himself, with some misgivings, submitted to this treatment but to no avail, since as he suspected, his pleural cavity was so full of adhesions that the gas could not penetrate enough to be of any help.

Pneumothorax did prove helpful to patients whose tuberculosis was fairly well localized, particularly in the upper lobe of one lung.

It was less successful with cases such as Trudeau's, where the disease was more extensive. Still, it became a valuable and standard treatment and was used for twenty years and more, until new surgical techniques could be perfected. One of the first of these, sometimes used in conjunction with pneumothorax, was the phrenic-nerve operation, a simple one to perform. One of the phrenic nerves, which control the movement of the diaphragm, was crushed or even removed to rest the lung during breathing. In Trudeau's time, it never occurred to the doctors at Saranac to consider removing pieces of the ribs in order to reduce the size of the chest cavity and put the lung at rest—a procedure that later became practicable.

While he gave up his practice entirely, now that his own health became more precarious, he continued to direct research and handle a voluminous correspondence. He entertained visitors in his home in the large paneled living room, and scarcely a week passed without some important individual as a guest.

Frequently he was asked to give talks, to tell the history of his work. Although he seldom complied with these requests, he made special efforts in certain instances. When in 1903, the financier Henry Phipps announced that he would endow an institute in Philadelphia to serve the cause, Trudeau accepted his invitation to open the annual series of lectures.

As he entered the auditorium and saw how large it was, packed with physicians and laymen, their eyes turned on him expectantly, he thought about his early fiasco at Baltimore. How had he gotten himself into this? These people looked at him as if they were about to hear a sermon from on high! The introduction was brief, fortunately, and when he arose to speak, he forgot his stage fright.

"Thirty years ago," he began in a clear though not loud voice, "when I went into the Adirondack wilderness to try to prolong my life, nothing would have seemed more improbable than that I should have lived to avail myself of the great honor of addressing you on this occasion, or that I might be worthy of your attention tonight."

He traced the development of his own knowledge about tuberculosis since 1873 and the struggle to establish his sanatorium. He talked about the laboratory and his continuing search for a cure or a vaccine. He spoke of Stevenson, of the small lamp in the wilderness whose light now spread around the world. He told the audience that 66 per cent of the incipient cases they had treated at the sanatorium were still in good health—showing the importance of early diagnosis and sanatorium care. What a contrast this was to the time, twenty-five years ago, when over the hospital-ward doors for consumptives could be written: *All hope abandon ye that enter here.*

Again he quoted the statement, "Cure sometimes, relieve often, comfort always." He concluded with the remark that, "We must look with hope, hope for increased knowledge to aid us in our struggle."

With applause ringing in his ears he returned once again to his beloved Saranac to work, no longer alone, but with Dr. Baldwin, Dr. Brown and other able men in his long, persistent search.

This was fortunate indeed, since physicians and Public Health men by the dozens now came to see the Adirondack Cottage Sanitarium to consult its founder. While Trudeau seldom went out for a meal when he was at home, he and Lottie had guests at their table nearly every evening. Usually Dr. Baldwin and Dr. Brown were present to join in the afterdinner discussions.

It was during one of these evenings that plans were made for the establishment of the American Sanatorium Association—an organization that would weld the growing number of these institutions into a progressive movement. Later this association was renamed the American Trudeau Society and made a part of the National Tuberculosis Association. When the men first began discussing the possibility, there were ninety-six such hospitals in the country. Four years later, in December, 1905, and three years after the association held its first meeting, the number had increased to 184. Bed capacity rose to fourteen thousand. But Trudeau still hoped for a nation-wide organization, which would include laymen as well as physicians.

Although he could not take an active part in the preliminary organization work, he spearheaded the movement through papers which were read for him at important medical meetings. Since 1901 he had been assuring physicians that 75 per cent of the cases of pulmonary consumption could be expected to recover if they were only recognized in time and placed in favorable surroundings. And he continued to insist that this was true.

Many of his colleagues in various parts of the country doubted it. As Dr. William Osler later remarked, "This was an extraordinary statement for the time."

Trudeau knew this as well as anyone, but he believed that he was right and that he must somehow shock people into action. He also decried the dependence on the sputum test as the chief means of diagnosing tuberculosis. Minimal or incipient cases often had no bacilli in their sputum. When Dr. Brown pointed out the storm of ridicule this statement brought from eminent physicians, Trudeau waved his hands in the air and said in a weary voice, "They will come around to it. As long as I have a breath of life I shall repeat this statement. They must seek out the cases in the first stages of phthisis."

After several false starts the National Association for the Study and Prevention of Tuberculosis was organized, with Trudeau as its first president.

The name of this new organization was itself meaningful, since it included the word "prevention," and meant that the new society would include community education among laymen and by laymen as well as by physicians, in addition to scientific study. Trudeau as well as the other founders were insistent on this point, and it undoubtedly contributed greatly to the association's success. A few years later the name was shortened to National Tuberculosis Association but it has never lost sight of its original purpose.

Trudeau traveled to Washington, D.C., to address the gathering in July, 1905. Again he insisted that "the first and greatest need is education. Education should begin by teaching in the public schools the main facts relating to the transmission of tuberculosis. Early detection of the disease is the first requisite for success in its treatment."

Great though the honor was—the presidency of the National Association—for his purposes the election as president for the

United States of the Sixth International Congress on Tuberculosis
was greater, for this was an older organization and would receive
a wide press at its meeting in Washington in 1908. Five thousand
delegates were registered. As he took his seat on the platform,
preparatory to addressing the large meeting, he learned that the
seat next to him was to be taken by Dr. Robert Koch. Suddenly he
heard a lowering of voices in the hall, followed by a low buzz of
whispers. Dr. Koch strutted across the platform and took his seat.

Trudeau held out his hand to the visitor. "Dr. Koch, this is a
great pleasure and honor."

The German bowed slightly. "I thank you. The honor is mine."

Trudeau relaxed and began to talk at a quick pace, sketching his
experience following Koch's first announcement about the discovery
of the bacillus. He described his meager equipment, his ignorance,
his trip to New York.

While he was speaking, Koch listened attentively, an amused
and quizzical smile on his face.

There was no more time for talking. The meeting was called to
order.

All that day and for many days after his return to Saranac,
Trudeau wondered what was going on in Koch's mind. Had the
great scientist known that many physicians in the audience longed
to ask why he still insisted that he could *cure* tuberculosis by injec-
tion?

The red-letter day of Trudeau's life was the twenty-fifth anniver-
sary of the establishment of his sanatorium. On February 14, 1910,
he and Lottie traveled along the snow-covered mountain road to
watch a series of pantomimes depicting the history of the institution.
As he looked at it now, his memory raced back to that day when he
stood so proudly before his almost-finished first building. There
were more than fifty—dotted all over the former pasture—valued at
more than a million dollars. The endowment was half a million
dollars and still growing. Under the snow were the shaded walks,
flower-bordered in summer. Only one thing remained the same—
the view of the mountains with the shifting clouds, the dark forest,

the snowy peaks and the bracing air. The wide verandas were there, but not a single patient could be seen. All were inside, waiting for him to enter the large lounge to watch their "show."

Paul Smith and good old Fitz were the lone survivors of that early day. The old crowd of guides and strong men he knew at St. Regis during his first years in the north woods were gone. His mother had died ten years ago. His sister Adelina, whom he had seen only briefly in New York, was dead; so was Luis Walton. What a depressing day this could have been had he allowed himself to think of all these departed friends, but the patients sang and smiled and performed their pantomimes with joy and verve. As he sat there he kept saying to himself, "Yes, that is just how it was."

At the end Fitz and the superintendent, Mr. Riddle, led him to the front.

"How can I find words to express my feelings?" he asked the audience. "When I came to the Adirondacks my life seemed hopeless, but the asset I had, which carried me through, was a good wife—the best wife that any man ever had."

Truly, did any man ever have such a reward for work?

Other rewards were to follow. The greatest—from a public and professional view—was the presidency of the Congress of American Physicians and Surgeons, the top honor open to a man of medicine in the United States. On May 4, 1910, he was strong enough to appear in person to give his presidential address.

Edward Livingston Trudeau was close to becoming a myth now. He was painfully thin as he walked down the aisle, and his back was kicking up again. He had other troubles. Halfway to the platform, he caught a glimpse of his old friend from Boston, seated on the aisle. He bent low and whispered in his ear: "Bowditch, don't ever have cystitis. I've written most of this address early in the morning when I could not sleep from pain."

He smiled at the astonished look on the face of Vincent Bowditch, and walked to the platform.

His voice was weak as he began his address:

"I have been sorely puzzled in the selection of a topic for my address to you tonight. I preferred not to impose on a general

Congress of Physicians and Surgeons a subject relating to my own specialty; I had not confidence enough in my powers, and too much consideration for you to attempt a more or less ambitious review of the advances and possibilities of medical science, so I finally decided simply to look back on the personal experiences of my own medical life and select from them some topic on which to say a few words to you.

"As I look back in my medical life, the one thing that seems to stand out as having been most helpful to me, and which has enabled me more than anything else to accomplish whatever I have been able to do, seems to me to have been that I was ever possessed of a large fund of optimism; indeed, at times optimism was about the only resource I had . . .

"Optimism is a product of a man's heart rather than of his head; and on that account is rather frowned upon by many physicians whose scientific training naturally leads them to depend solely upon the qualities of the intellect, and look with suspicion upon any product of the emotions."

He stopped for a moment to catch his breath. Again he spoke to the waiting audience.

"The scientist without optimism may be an admirable intellectual machine, who it is true is not likely to be led astray from the well-worn road of demonstrable and generally already demonstrated facts, and as such he will have his place in life; but he will never climb above the ruck, he will create and achieve little in the field of original research unless faith in his own powers furnishes the incentive to constant effort, and imagination leads him into an unexplored region, to new methods, untried lines of investigation.

"The professor of medicine and the laboratory director need optimism if they are to inspire their students to do their best work, and they should beware how they quench, too often unfortunately with ridicule, the optimism of the young men who look to them for direction. Overenthusiasm is not a serious fault in a young man and can easily be kept within bounds, and optimism in a student is a better incentive to work than pessimism.

"The practicing physician and surgeon must have optimism if he is to develop a full degree of efficiency in meeting the terrible emergencies of acute illness and accidents, or the long-drawn-out struggle with lingering and hopeless disease, and at the same time inspire his patients with a degree of optimism which means everything to them in the ordeals they have to pass through. To the practicing physician and surgeon optimism is even more necessary than to the scientist. In his hour of need the patient has no means of judging of the physician's intellectual attainments; it is faith that radiates from the doctor's personality that he seizes upon and that is helpful to him.

"The conquest of disease by prevention, though disease is the source of the doctor's livelihood, the placing ever at the disposal of the poor without money and without price the greatest gifts of learning and skill at our command, the strangling of deception and quackery in our midst by education of the people, are standards which can only be inaugurated and upheld by the highest type of optimism.

"Let us not, therefore, quench the faith or turn from the vision. Thus inspired, many will reach the goal; and if for most of us our achievements inevitably must fall far short of our ideals, if when age and infirmity overtake us 'we come not within sight of the castles of our dreams,' nevertheless all will be well with us; for does not Stevenson tell us rightly that 'to travel hopefully is better than to arrive, and the true success is in labor'?"

Trudeau's voice had grown weaker and weaker as he approached the closing paragraphs of his address. Only those in the front of the hall were able to hear all that he said, but when he reached the end, everyone present stood and clapped. As Trudeau proceeded up the aisle, all turned toward him, many reaching out their hands to his. The nation's doctors assembled for this address had become familiar with the legends surrounding the scientist and practicing physician who spoke to them. They were familiar with his work as leading exponent of the sanatorium theory, and his pronouncements on the subject of public health. They now looked on him in still another focus. They watched the retreating figure and knew that here was, also, a philosopher.

XIX.

FINAL YEARS

◻◼◻

Trudeau made no more public appearances, but he still had work
to do and felt very much a part of the outside world.

A great deal of sentiment against experimentation with animals
arose at this time, and he felt impelled to defend his colleagues
against sentimental attackers. "Thanks to animal experimentation,"
he told a reporter, "we know today that tuberculosis is not inherited,
that it is communicable and therefore preventable, and that in its
earlier stages it is curable. Animal experimentation has taught us
much as to the different types of tubercle bacillus, its virulence, the
poisons it produces, and the manner in which it invades the living
organism and destroys it."

When he learned of some new "sure cure" he lashed out in indignation to prevent gullible people from raising false hopes among the
tuberculous. A few words from Edward Livingston Trudeau, appear-
ing in the New York *Times*, were enough to discredit any of these
false claims among discerning readers. Fakers themselves kept clear
of Saranac Lake.

This "city of the sick" was still the beacon, the guiding spirit, in
the struggle against tuberculosis. The entire area became known as
a health resort—the Endicott Johnson Corporation, the DuPont
Company, the National Variety Artists and other organizations
established sanatoria in the Adirondacks. Large privately operated
institutions such as Stony Wold, Gabriels, and numerous small
nursing homes were built to house the patients. The United States
Veterans Administration erected a large tuberculosis hospital near
Saranac Lake.

As so often happens when a man achieves fame, extravagant

claims were made about Trudeau's work, and he was disturbed about it.

Trudeau referred to these statements one day when he was speaking to Dr. Allen Krause of Baltimore, who had come to see him. "Why, there are dozens of physicians who have worked as hard and effectively as I. Some have done better. Really, Krause, I am a failure! The search to which I devoted thirty years of my life is as far away as ever. We still have no vaccine."

"Well, so we haven't," Dr. Krause replied. "That is no reason to call yourself a failure. Have you forgotten that even in nineteen-four almost a hundred and ninety out of each hundred thousand people in our country died of tuberculosis? Now, in nineteen-fourteen, we have cut that down to a hundred and twenty-five, according to the best estimates. Your work up here spearheaded the drive. You can't expect to turn a miracle."

A miracle. That was exactly what he had hoped to do. These were his own words. Krause was right. Miracles in medicine seldom come from one man or from one laboratory. Even Koch worked on data supplied by his early teacher. A genuine cure for tuberculosis would be the result of the toil of many scientists in many laboratories working painstakingly, often unknown, toward this goal. The discovery would not come until scientists achieved a sufficient backlog of knowledge. One man might—in the public's mind—be called the "discoverer," but the real credit would belong to thousands who through trial and error made the final victory possible. Perhaps his own work here in his laboratories might be useful in paving the way.

For several years physicians and other friends had been urging him to write the story of his life or allow someone else to do it for him. Usually his answer was, "Why write my life? I'm too busy to think about it."

Now that he could no longer practice and the administration of the sanatorium was in capable hands, requiring little advice from him, he began to consider the idea. He rejected the suggestion that he allow someone else to tell his story. It was sure to be unrealistic. No one, however skilled, could draw a true picture of another's life.

One argument finally convinced him that he should do it himself: it would provide inspiration to other young men who were starting careers with only average education and promise.

"As I look back on my life since 1866 when my brother came to me sick at Newport, tuberculosis looms up as an ever-present and relentless foe," he wrote.

At times during these early months of 1914, he was so weak that he could not write without great effort. If only he could go hunting with Fitz and Francis as he had done only two years ago. The memory of those happy days spurred him on, and his only son gave him daily encouragement.

Francis, now a physician, graduated from Johns Hopkins, was not to be argued out of setting up his practice in Saranac Lake, and neither his father nor mother attempted to do so. He was a constant joy to them, with his strapping, athletic figure, his gay, kindly disposition, his earnest regard for the traditions his father established.

Just a year after Francis brought his bride, the former Helen Garretson of Morristown, New Jersey, to the Adirondacks in July, 1914, the family journeyed to the little church in the wilderness to watch the christening of their first grandchild—Edward Livingston Trudeau. It was a beautiful day, and as Dr. Baldwin stood at the altar with the young parents to take his vows as the baby's godfather, Trudeau thought of the many happy hours, and the few sad ones, he had spent in this log chapel. How strange it seemed that this son Francis, born late in the lives of his parents, should be the only one left to carry on the tradition.

As he and Lottie left the chapel he said, "Tuberculosis has robbed us of a lot, I know. But it has given me experiences that I cherish too. I would not exchange these for the wealth of the Indies!"

"A spiritual wealth, yes it has."

As he worked on his autobiography, Trudeau gave considerable thought to this problem of failure with which he had argued with Dr. Krause. He had spoken foolishly, selfishly. Man must accept failures. He cannot reach all his goals. In one thing, one aim he felt that he had succeeded. "I have learned that the conquest of

Fate is not by struggling against it, not trying to escape from it, but by acquiescence. God only can judge our failures."

One evening as Lottie sat with him in the twilight, he turned his head on the pillow and reach for her hand. "The book is finished, and I've burned all my private correspondence so you won't be bothered with it."

His voice was weak now, and he spent most of his time in bed.

"I am content to await patiently the end of the great Mystery of Existence, for I still have your love, and that is the best of all possessions. That and faith."

He did not have long to wait. Edward Livingston Trudeau died on Tuesday, November 15, 1915, soon after he finished proofreading his *Autobiography*.

The nation paused in its preoccupation with news of the war. The New York *Times* gave almost the entire front page to his picture and story, and published an editorial, "A Glory of Science Has Departed." The Baltimore *News* pointed out that there were now five hundred sanatoria in the United States and Canada, representing "one of the greatest revolutions of the century." The New York *Herald* said, "With the death of Dr. Edward L. Trudeau this country loses the man who taught the world more about tuberculosis than any other of this generation." And the New York *Globe* summed up, saying that "To humanity Dr. Trudeau brought relief from suffering and hopelessness. Of even more value was the lesson of passionate devotion to a single simple idea that lies at the root of human happiness."

Trudeau's *Autobiography* received the widespread attention of the general public, and through the years has been read by most "curetakers." It is now in its fifth edition.

Lottie stayed on in the square frame house, giving her waning strength to church work, happy to watch her daughter-in-law, Helen, take over her duties at the sanatorium, providing clothing for the needy, decorating the rooms with chintz curtains and brightly colored cushions, a watchful, charming wife for a busy doctor. A new grandson, named Francis Jr., was born and now the fine old house rang with the laughter of children once more. Lottie died in 1923.

The Adirondack Cottage Sanitarium continued to grow in influence until in 1955 it closed its doors—in happy recognition of discoveries in chemistry which shortened the duration of "cures" and made them easier in any climate, in any town. The research laboratory, now a well-endowed institution, renamed for Trudeau, is still operating, still searching for the vaccine its founder so long sought. The sanatorium buildings have been taken over by the American Management Association as a training school for young executives.

Saranac Lake is changing in character, becoming famous once again as a sports center, but the tradition of charity, compassion and devotion to patients lives on in a young, able, energetic and kindly Dr. Francis B. Trudeau, Jr., who came to take over the practice of his father, who died in 1957. He and his family have a long, rambling house at the top of Mount Pisgah, above the old sanatorium grounds, where they can sit and look out at Whiteface Mountain and the ranges beyond, watching as did Edward Livingston Trudeau the changing lights and shadows of a winter afternoon.

BIBLIOGRAPHY

Atkinson, W. M., ed. *The Physicians and Surgeons of the United States.* Philadelphia, 1878.

Brown, Lawrason. *Story of Clinical Pulmonary Tuberculosis.* Baltimore, 1941.

Brown, L., and others. *Edward Livingston Trudeau, a Symposium.* New York, 1935.

Chalmers, Stephen. *The Beloved Physician.* New York, 1915.

Chalmers, S. *The Penny Piper of Saranac.* Boston, 1916.

Cole, Elizabeth. *Fifty Years at Trudeau Sanatorium.* Trudeau, New York, 1935.

Cummins, S. L. *Tuberculosis in History from the Seventeenth Century. . . .* London, 1949.

Cushing, Harvey. *Life of Sir William Osler.* Oxford, 1925. 2 vols.

Donaldson, A. L. *A History of the Adirondacks.* New York, 1921. 2 vols.

Dubos, René and Jean. *The White Plague.* Boston, 1952.

Flick, E. M. *Beloved Crusader.* Philadelphia, 1944.

Hallock, G., and C. E. Turner. *Edward Livingston Trudeau.* Boston, 1929.

Hooker, Mildred P. Stokes. *Camp Chronicles.* Privately printed, n.d.

Kennon, George E. *Edward H. Harriman.* New York, 1922. 2 vols.

Long, E. *Funny Sayings of the Late Paul Smith.* New York, 1913.

Muller, James Arthur. *The Religion of Dr. Trudeau.*

Myers, J. A. *Fighters of Fate.* Baltimore, 1927.

Raymond, H. *The Story of Saranac.* New York, 1909.

Riley, Lester L. *The Chronicle of Little Neck and Douglaston, Long Island.* New York, 1936.

Sesquicentennial Issue, *New York State Journal of Medicine, 1807-1957.* New York, Feb. 1, 1957.

Shrady, J., ed. *College of Physicians and Surgeons of New York.* New York, 1902. 2 vols.

188 BIBLIOGRAPHY

Shryock, Richard H. *National Tuberculosis Association*, 1904-1954. New York, 1957.

Titus, J. H. *Adirondack Pioneers*. Troy, N.Y., 1899.

Townsend, R. T. *The Mother of Clubs . . . Union Club, 1836-1936*. New York, 1936.

Trudeau, Edward Livingston. *An Autobiography*. 5th Edition, New York, 1951.

American Review of Tuberculosis, Journal of the Outdoor Life, and other publications of the National Tuberculosis Association, including pamphlets; magazines and proceedings of various medical associations and foundations in the United States and Europe. Files of the New York *Times* and other city newspapers; *Adirondack Daily Enterprise*, Saranac Lake, New York. Articles of general interest about Dr. Trudeau and the sanatorium listed in the *Reader's Guide to Periodic Literature*. Copies of articles by Trudeau are in the files of the National Tuberculosis Association and in the library of the Trudeau Foundation, Saranac Lake. The Trudeau Collection of family papers and memorabilia are in the Saranac Free Library. Information on the Beare family and Dr. Trudeau is available in the Zion Episcopal Church, Douglaston, Long Island Collection. The Union Club Library, the libraries of the Long Island Historical Society, Brooklyn, the New York Academy of Medicine, the King's County Medical Society, all have material on Trudeau and the tuberculosis movement. The largest collection on the sanatorium is in the Trudeau Foundation Collection, Saranac Lake.

INDEX

◻◻◻